Oster®

Creative
Entertaining
Simple to Sophisticated

Publications International, Ltd.

Pictured on the front cover: Goat Cheese Stuffed Figs *(page 58)*.
Pictured on the back cover (clockwise from top): Espresso Mousse *(page 106)*, Seared Beef Tenderloin with Horseradish-Rosemary Cream *(page 130)*, and Jumbo Lump Crabmeat with Potato Pancakes, Mango and Baby Greens *(page 64)*.

ISBN-13: 978-1-4127-9941-6
ISBN-10: 1-4127-9941-4

Library of Congress Control Number: 2007941639

Manufactured in China.

8 7 6 5 4 3 2 1

Table of Contents

**Creative Entertaining
Is Easy with Oster® Products**   **4**

An Outdoor Affair   **6**
Throw a perfect backyard party with grilled appetizers and entrées, fresh sides and desserts, and fabulous blended drinks.

Stylish at Sunup   **34**
Wake up with creative waffles, pancakes, breakfast casseroles, and smoothies.

Sophisticated Entertaining   **58**
These elegant appetizers, entrées, sides, and desserts will turn your kitchen and dining room into a five-star restaurant.

Family Celebrations   **82**
The kids, the great-grandparents, and everyone in between will love these fun recipes, great for birthday parties and other family gatherings.

Casual Elegance   **106**
Forget the take-out pizza—make movie night more special with these delicious snacks and main dishes.

Holiday Cool   **130**
Preparing the most anticipated meals of the year is simple and stress-free with these festive recipes.

Index   **154**

18

78

68

Creative Entertaining
Is Easy with Oster® Products

The word "entertaining" can be intimidating. It conjures images of formal gatherings and difficult dishes, of stressful dinner parties spent running in circles. The idea of entertaining can make even the most seasoned home cook nervous. It doesn't have to.

There is a certain virtue in simplicity. Good food, enjoyed with good friends, makes for the best celebrations. These simple get-togethers are made even easier with Oster® appliances. *Creative Entertaining* contains recipes perfect for common entertaining occasions, ranging from casual Sunday brunches to elaborate holiday dinners. Whether you're hosting a backyard barbecue or an elegant cocktail party, there are a few key ideas for throwing a successful soirée. However, none are more important than understanding that entertaining is a matter of balance.

• **Pick the entrée first**
Pick your main course first—it is the main course, after all—then select the rest of your menu to complement it. Planning sides and desserts is easy when you've already made the biggest decision.

• **Balance flavors, textures, and temperatures of food**
After selecting your main course, build a plan for the other foods you'll serve. Choose a wide variety of tastes, textures, and temperatures—this allows for interesting flavor combinations, and also increases your chances of serving foods that appeal to all of your guests. Furthermore, selecting foods that are served at different temperatures reduces the need to cook multiple dishes at the same time.

• **Cook what you enjoy eating**
Yes, you've invited guests to a party and you want them to be happy with the menu, but that doesn't mean you can't pick dishes based on what you like. You

get to pick the frosting on your own birthday cake, don't you? Why should this be any different? You're throwing the party, so if you want rice pilaf instead of stuffing with your roast chicken, serve it!

• Consider a themed party
Make a birthday or holiday party even more memorable by choosing a theme. Dazzle your guests with an evening in Morocco: mail invitations on card stock in rich, earthy colors, use vibrantly patterned scarves as table runners, and decorate a buffet table with brightly colored tiles and white candles in brass holders. Start the evening off right with Moroccan Chicken Turnovers *(page 66)* and keep the party going with Lemon Chicken with Moroccan Olives, Pine Nuts, Toasted Garlic and Couscous *(page 70)*.

Or, celebrate Cinco de Mayo with a Mexican buffet: use a sombrero as a centerpiece, scatter chili peppers on the table for color, and use individual clay pots for smaller dishes and fixings. Greet your guests at the door with Frozen Margaritas *(page 12)*. Don't forget the music!

• Pay attention to presentation
The way a meal is served is a fun and interesting variable in entertaining. The same menu can feel formal or casual depending on how the dishes are presented. For example, Garlic Shrimp Casserole *(page 97)* can be individually plated in the kitchen and served to seated guests if the boss is coming over for dinner. Or, for a get-together with the new neighbors, serve the casserole family-style with Honey-Lemon Green & Yellow Beans *(page 100)*, letting guests serve themselves from platters passed around the table. The possibilities are endless!

edamame hummus

1 package (**16 ounces**) frozen shelled edamame, thawed

2 green onions, roughly chopped (about ½ cup)

½ cup loosely packed fresh cilantro

3 to 4 tablespoons water

2 tablespoons canola oil

1½ tablespoons fresh lime juice

1 tablespoon honey

2 cloves garlic

1 teaspoon salt

¼ teaspoon black pepper

Rice crackers, baby carrots, cucumber slices and sugar snap peas

Place edamame, green onions, cilantro, 3 tablespoons water, oil, lime juice, honey, garlic, salt and pepper in Oster® Food Processor; process until smooth. Add additional water if necessary to thin out and smooth dip.

Serve with crackers and vegetables for dipping. Store leftover dip in refrigerator up to 4 days.

tangerine tequila shrimp

MAKES 6 SERVINGS

2 pounds raw (31 to 40 per pound size) shrimp, cleaned and deveined
½ cup packed fresh cilantro leaves
1 large dried red California chili, cut in half
½ red onion, cut into 4 pieces
2 fresh green chilies, cut in half (stems removed)
4 tangerines,* peeled and cut in half (seeds removed)
1 teaspoon grated lime peel
⅓ cup fresh lime juice (about 2 large limes)
1 teaspoon cumin seeds
2 tablespoons orange-flavored liqueur (optional)
¼ cup tequila
1 tablespoon olive oil
3 cloves garlic
1 teaspoon sea salt
3 tablespoons turbinado sugar (raw cane sugar)

Place shrimp on bamboo skewers. Lay skewered shrimp in flat container with tight-fitting lid.

Place remaining ingredients in order listed in Oster® Blender jar. Cover jar with lid. Press POWER, then press FROZEN DRINK. Press START/STOP. Pour marinade all over shrimp, cover container and marinate 15 minutes in the refrigerator.

Preheat grill. Remove skewered shrimp from marinade and grill 2 minutes on each side.

Note: May be served with prepared guacamole and/or salsa for dipping.

*Tangelos and clementines also work well but if none are available you may substitute 1 can (16 ounces) mandarin orange slices, drained.

An Outdoor Affair

cuban-style marinated skirt steak

MAKES 6 SERVINGS

2	**pounds beef skirt steak, cut into 6-inch pieces**
2	**cups orange juice, divided**
½	**cup lemon juice**
½	**cup lime juice**
¼	**cup olive oil**
5	**cloves garlic, minced**
1	**teaspoon dried oregano**
1	**large onion, halved and thinly sliced**
2	**teaspoons grated orange peel, plus additional for garnish**
3	**cups cooked white rice**
3	**cups cooked black beans**

Place steaks in large resealable food storage bag. Mix 1 cup orange juice, lemon juice, lime juice, oil, garlic and oregano in small bowl; set aside ½ cup. Pour remaining juice mixture over steaks. Seal bag, turn to coat. Marinate in refrigerator 30 minutes.

Combine remaining 1 cup orange juice, onion and 2 teaspoons orange peel in separate small bowl; set aside.

Prepare grill for direct cooking. Remove steaks from marinade; discard marinade. Place steaks on grid over high heat. Grill, covered, 6 to 10 minutes or until desired doneness, turning once. Let stand; cover with tented foil 5 minutes before slicing.

Slice meat across the grain into thin slices. Transfer to serving platter. Remove onions from orange juice; arrange on top of meat. Sprinkle with reserved juice mixture and additional orange peel. Serve with rice and black beans.

Oster

Entertaining Tip

Ensure the best results every time by using an Oster® Rice Cooker. The airtight lid locks in moisture.

An Outdoor Affair

frozen margarita

MAKES 4 SERVINGS

½ **cup gold tequila**

¼ **cup orange-flavored cognac or liqueur**

2 **tablespoons fresh lime juice, plus additional for rimming glasses**

¼ **cup sugar**

3 **cups ice**

Salt, for rimming glasses

Combine ingredients except salt in order listed in Oster® Blender jar. Cover jar with lid, press POWER, then select FROZEN DRINKS. Press START/STOP.

Coat rims of stemmed glasses with lime juice, then dip in salt. Pour drinks into prepared glasses.

Note: If desired, granulated sugar can be used in place of salt.

frozen sunshine

MAKES 4 SERVINGS

½ **cup vodka**

¼ **cup clear orange-flavored liqueur**

¼ **cup half-and-half**

¼ **cup frozen orange juice concentrate**

4 **cups ice**

4 **orange slices (optional)**

4 **paper umbrellas (optional)**

Place ingredients in order listed in Oster® Blender jar. Cover jar with lid. Press POWER, then press FROZEN DRINKS. Press START/STOP. Pour into stemmed glasses. Garnish with orange slices and paper umbrellas as desired.

Oster

Entertaining Tip

If you can't make it to Mexico for the real thing, why not throw your own Mexican-themed party? Think bold and vivacious. Music should be fun and upbeat.

FROZEN MARGARITA

thai cabbage-apple slaw

MAKES 6 TO 8 SERVINGS

2	Gala apples, cored and cut into matchsticks
3	cups shredded green cabbage
¼	cup rice vinegar
1	tablespoon sugar
1	teaspoon soy sauce
2	tablespoons vegetable oil
½	teaspoon sesame oil
¼	teaspoon salt
2	tablespoons sesame seeds, toasted
2	tablespoons chopped peanuts

Combine apples and cabbage in large bowl. Whisk together vinegar, sugar, soy sauce, both oils and salt in separate bowl. Pour over salad and toss well to combine. Refrigerate several hours or overnight (but not more than 12 hours) to allow flavors to blend. Garnish with sesame seeds and peanuts.

grilled potato salad

MAKES 4 SERVINGS

DRESSING

4 **tablespoons country Dijon mustard**

1 **tablespoon white wine or apple cider vinegar**

3 **tablespoons olive oil**

2 **tablespoons chopped dill weed**

½ **teaspoon salt**

¼ **teaspoon black pepper**

SALAD

1 **teaspoon salt**

2 **pounds small red potatoes**

2 **tablespoons olive oil**

1 **large sheet foil**

1 **green onion, thinly sliced**

Combine all dressing ingredients in glass measuring cup. Stir with fork to blend well; set aside.

Preheat grill to medium-high. Bring 8 cups water and salt to a boil. Cut potatoes into ½-inch slices. Add potatoes to water; boil about 5 minutes. Drain into colander. Transfer potatoes to bowl; drizzle with olive oil and toss lightly.

Spray 1 side of foil with cooking spray. Transfer potatoes to foil; fold into a packet. Place potato packet on grid over medium-high heat. Grill 7 to 10 minutes or until potatoes are tender. Transfer potatoes to serving bowl. Sprinkle with green onion. Toss gently with reserved dressing. Serve warm.

Oster

Entertaining Tip

Grilling starchy vegetables, like potatoes, in foil packets helps cook them evenly. Just use care when opening packets; pierce the foil with a sharp knife and allow steam to escape before unwrapping packets all the way.

frozen mojito

MAKES 6 SERVINGS

½ cup lime juice

1 to 2 drops green food coloring (optional)

1 cup fresh mint leaves

½ cup sugar

¼ cup light rum

2 cups ice

1 cup water

Lime slices and fresh mint leaves, for garnish (optional)

Place all ingredients except garnish in the order listed in Oster® Blender jar. Blend until smooth. Pour immediately into chilled glasses. Garnish with lime slices and whole mint leaves as desired.

frozen daiquiri

MAKES 4 (6-OUNCE) SERVINGS

⅓ cup frozen limeade concentrate

5 ice cubes

4½ ounces (½ cup plus 1 tablespoon) light rum

Blend in Oster® Blender until mixture has consistency of soft sherbet. Do not strain.

Oster

Entertaining Tip

This famous frosty combination of limeade, rum and crushed ice is easily blended to the proper consistency in an Oster® Blender.

FROZEN MOJITO

chilled avocado & gazpacho soup

MAKES ABOUT 8 SERVINGS

4	**Mexican Haas avocados, peeled and seeded, plus additional diced avocado for garnish**
	Pinch ground cumin
2	**cups vegetable or chicken broth, cold**
2	**tablespoons lime juice**
2	**tablespoons chopped fresh cilantro, plus additional for garnish**
	Salt and black pepper
4	**beefsteak tomatoes, chopped**
6	**cucumbers, peeled and chopped**
6	**red peppers, seeded and diced**
2	**cloves garlic**
1	**Spanish onion, peeled and chopped**
1	**cup tomato juice**
1	**tablespoon sherry vinegar**
2	**tablespoons extra-virgin oil**
1	**pound lobster meat, chilled and shelled**

Purée avocados, cumin, broth, lime juice and cilantro in Oster® Blender until smooth. Season to taste with salt and pepper. Refrigerate avocado soup until ready to serve.

Purée tomatoes, cucumbers, red peppers, garlic, Spanish onion, tomato juice, vinegar and olive oil in Oster® Blender until smooth. Refrigerate gazpacho until ready to serve.

Pour scant ½ cup avocado soup and gazpacho into chilled soup bowl; pour soups into opposite sides of bowl but allow to mix in bottom of bowl. Garnish with about 2 ounces chilled lobster meat, and sprinkle with chopped cilantro and diced avocado, as desired.

grilled vegetable salad
with feta and olives

MAKES 4 TO 6 SERVINGS

Combine lemon juice, broth, extra-virgin olive oil, tomatoes and oregano in Oster® Blender or Oster® Food Processor. Pulse until smooth. Season to taste with salt and pepper.

Lightly brush eggplant, fennel, zucchini, onion and lemon slices with olive oil and grill on Oster® Indoor Grill or outdoor grill until brown and tender. Transfer to serving dish and gently toss with some of prepared dressing.

Toss salad greens, feta and olives in remaining dressing and arrange on large platter. Layer grilled vegetables on top, season with additional salt and pepper as desired, and serve.

Note: This bounty of Mediterranean vegetables makes a delicious heart-healthy meal.

3	tablespoons fresh lemon juice
3	tablespoons chicken broth
1½	tablespoons extra-virgin olive oil
2	plum tomatoes, chopped
1	teaspoon dried oregano
	Salt and black pepper
1	small eggplant, sliced
1	fennel bulb, trimmed and sliced
2	small zucchini, sliced
1	red onion, sliced
1	lemon, sliced
2	tablespoons olive oil
2	cups mixed salad greens
¾	cup (3 ounces) crumbled feta cheese
½	cup kalamata olives

nutty toffee ice cream cake

MAKES 12 SERVINGS

1 package (18¼ ounces) devil's food cake mix, plus ingredients to prepare mix

2 quarts vanilla ice cream, slightly softened

1½ cups toffee baking bits, divided

1 container (14 ounces) cream-filled pirouette cookies (about 30 cookies)

1 container (16 ounces) chocolate frosting

¾ cup unsalted peanuts or nut topping, toasted and chopped

Ribbon (optional)

Spray 2 (9-inch) round cake pans with nonstick cooking spray. Prepare cake mix, pour into prepared pans and bake according to package directions. Cool in pans on wire racks 15 minutes. Remove from pans; cool completely on wire racks.

Place 1 cake layer on serving plate. Spread 4 cups softened ice cream evenly over cake. Sprinkle with ¾ cup toffee bits. Top with remaining cake layer. Spread remaining 4 cups ice cream evenly over cake. Wrap with plastic wrap coated with nonstick cooking spray; freeze about 30 minutes.

Meanwhile, carefully cut each cookie in half lengthwise with sharp serrated knife.

Remove cake from freezer. Frost side only with chocolate frosting. Place cookie halves vertically around side of cake. Sprinkle nuts and remaining ¾ cup toffee bits over top of cake. Wrap with plastic wrap; freeze overnight or at least 8 hours until very firm. Tie ribbon around cake before serving, if desired.

Variation: For a beautiful holiday look, substitute candy canes for pirouette cookies and crushed peppermint candies for nuts and toffee bits.

Oster

Entertaining Tip

To cut pretty, even slices, use an Oster® Electric Knife. Carefully dip knife blades in a tall glass of warm water and wipe dry between slices.

olive tapenade

MAKES 1¾ CUPS DIP

1 can (16 ounces) medium pitted black olives, drained
½ cup pimiento-stuffed green olives
1 tablespoon roasted garlic*
½ teaspoon dry mustard
½ cup (2 ounces) crumbled feta cheese
1 tablespoon olive oil
Toasted bread slices

Process olives, roasted garlic and mustard in Oster® Food Processor or Blender until finely chopped.

Combine olive mixture, feta cheese and oil in medium bowl; stir until well blended. Serve with toasted bread.

Oster

*To roast garlic, preheat oven to 400°F. Remove outer layers of papery skin and cut ¼ inch off top of garlic head. Place cut side up on a piece of heavy-duty foil. Drizzle with 2 teaspoons olive oil; wrap tightly in foil. Bake 25 to 30 minutes or until cloves feel soft when pressed. Cool slightly before squeezing out garlic pulp.

Entertaining Tip

For the best flavor, prepare this tapenade several hours or a day ahead to allow the flavors to blend.

grilled peaches
with nutmeg pastry cream

MAKES 4 SERVINGS

4	peaches, halved
	Cinnamon-sugar*
3	egg yolks
	Pinch salt
⅓	cup sugar
2	tablespoons all-purpose flour
1¼	cups whole milk
1	teaspoon vanilla
	Pinch ground nutmeg
2	tablespoons butter
	Fresh mint sprigs (optional)
	Whipped topping (optional)

Sprinkle peach halves with cinnamon-sugar. Grill over medium-low heat just until tender and slightly golden brown. (Peaches should still be firm and hold shape.) Remove from grill. Set aside.

Combine egg yolks, salt, sugar and flour in medium bowl; stir until well blended.

Place milk, vanilla and nutmeg in medium saucepan; bring just to boiling over low to medium-low heat. Add some heated milk mixture to yolk mixture, whisking constantly.

Add egg yolk mixture to remaining milk in saucepan; whisking constantly until thick. Remove from heat and add butter; whisk until well blended.

Spoon sauce onto dessert plates; arrange peach halves on top of sauce. Garnish with mint sprig and whipped topping, if desired.

*To make cinnamon-sugar, combine 2 tablespoons sugar with 1 teaspoon ground cinnamon.

Oster

Entertaining Tip

Fruit kabobs are a fun way to end a meal. Cut fruit into 1-inch chunks and place on a skewer. Grill, uncovered, about 5 minutes or until the fruit is tender. Serve plain or with a sweet dip.

mascarpone-mint ice cream, fresh figs
and vanilla-lemon syrup

MAKES 4 SERVINGS

1¾	cups sugar
3	cups water
16	ounces mascarpone cheese
3	tablespoons lemon juice
15	fresh mint leaves, chopped
4	grapefruit sections
4	fresh figs, halved
	Vanilla-Lemon Syrup (recipe follows)

Bring sugar and water to boil, stirring until sugar is completely dissolved. Remove from heat and add mascarpone cheese, lemon juice and mint. Stir to thoroughly combine. Refrigerate and allow flavors to develop overnight.

Strain ice cream batter, then freeze in ice cream maker according to manufacturer's instructions.

Scoop ice cream into 4 serving bowls. Add 1 grapefruit section and 2 fig pieces to each. Drizzle with Vanilla-Lemon Syrup. Serve immediately.

vanilla-lemon syrup

1	cup sugar
1	cup water
2	vanilla beans, scraped (reserve seeds for another use)
	Lemon juice

Bring sugar, water and vanilla beans to a boil. Remove from heat and strain. Add lemon juice to taste.

strawberry-apricot barbecue cornish hens

MAKES 4 SERVINGS

Prepare grill for indirect grilling or preheat oven to 375°F. Remove skin from game hen halves or chicken leg quarters; discard.

Combine poultry seasoning, salt and pepper in small bowl; rub over hens. Place hens on grill rack or in 15 × 10-inch jelly-roll pan. Grill, covered, over indirect medium heat 40 minutes; or bake, uncovered, 40 minutes.

Meanwhile, combine strawberries, barbecue sauce and preserves in small saucepan; bring to a boil. Reduce heat; cover and simmer 10 minutes. Remove from heat. Mash strawberries. Return to a boil. Reduce heat. Simmer, uncovered, about 5 minutes or until of desired consistency.

Brush strawberry mixture over poultry. Continue grilling or baking 5 to 15 minutes longer or until temperature reads 180°F when measured with meat thermometer inserted into thickest part of thigh, not touching bone. Transfer game hen halves or chicken to serving platter. Serve with remaining strawberry mixture.

2 Cornish game hens (1 ¼ pounds each), split lengthwise, *or* 4 chicken leg quarters (about **14** ounces each)

½ tablespoon poultry seasoning

½ teaspoon salt

¼ teaspoon black pepper

1½ cups frozen unsweetened strawberries (about 6 ounces)

½ cup barbecue sauce

¼ cup sugar-free apricot preserves

An Outdoor Affair

steak al forno

MAKES 2 TO 3 SERVINGS

4 cloves garlic, minced
1 tablespoon olive oil
1 tablespoon coarse salt
1 teaspoon black pepper
2 porterhouse or T-bone steaks (about 1 to 1¼ inches thick)
¼ cup grated Parmesan cheese

Prepare grill for direct cooking. Combine garlic, olive oil, salt and pepper; press into both sides of steaks. Let stand 15 minutes.

Place steaks on grid over medium-high heat. Cover; grill 14 to 19 minutes or until internal temperature of steak reaches 145°F for medium-rare doneness, turning once. Sprinkle cheese over steaks during last minute of cooking.

Transfer steaks to carving board; tent with foil. Let stand 5 minutes. To serve, cut meat away from each side of bone. Cut boneless pieces into slices. Serve immediately.

Oster

Entertaining Tip

For a smoked flavor, soak 2 cups hickory or oak wood chips in cold water at least 30 minutes. Drain and scatter over hot coals before grilling.

chicken
with mango-cherry chutney

MAKES 4 SERVINGS

1½ cups chopped fresh
mangoes, divided
(about 2 large
mangoes)

⅓ cup dried tart cherries

1 tablespoon packed
brown sugar

1 tablespoon cider vinegar

½ teaspoon mustard
seeds, slightly crushed

¼ teaspoon salt, divided

¼ cup sliced green onions

1½ teaspoons Chinese
5-spice powder

4 boneless skinless
chicken breasts *or* 8
small boneless skinless
chicken thighs (about 1
pound total)

Prepare grill for direct cooking.

Combine ½ cup mango, cherries, brown sugar, vinegar, mustard seeds and ⅛ teaspoon salt in medium saucepan; cook and stir over medium-low heat 5 minutes or until mango is tender. Slightly mash mango. Stir in remaining 1 cup mango and onions. Keep chutney warm until serving.

Lightly sprinkle 5-spice powder and remaining ⅛ teaspoon salt on both sides of chicken. Grill chicken directly over medium heat 7 to 10 minutes or until chicken is no longer pink in center, turning once.

Serve mango mixture over chicken pieces.

Oster

Entertaining Tip

Chinese 5-spice powder is a blend of cinnamon, star anise, fennel seed, anise and ginger. It is available in most supermarkets and at Asian grocery stores.

mango-banana foster

MAKES 4 SERVINGS

2 medium mangoes, peeled, seeded and chopped

2 ripe, firm bananas, cut into ¾-inch-thick slices

8 maraschino cherries, halved

4 sheets (18 × 12 inches each) heavy-duty foil

½ cup packed brown sugar

2 tablespoons dark rum *or* 2 tablespoons orange juice plus ¼ teaspoon rum extract

½ teaspoon ground cinnamon

Vanilla ice cream

Prepare grill for direct cooking.

Place mango, banana and cherries in center of each piece of foil. Stir together brown sugar, rum and cinnamon in small bowl. Spoon brown sugar mixture over fruit mixture.

Double-fold sides and ends of foil to seal packets, leaving head space for heat circulation. Place on baking sheet.

Slide packets off baking sheet onto grid over medium-high heat. Grill, covered, 3 to 5 minutes or until hot. Carefully open one end of each packet to allow steam to escape.

Meanwhile, spoon ice cream into serving bowls. Open packets; pour fruit over ice cream.

Stylish at Sunup

morning mocha smoothie

MAKES 1 SERVING

½ cup fat-free milk	*Place* ingredients in order given into Oster® Blender jar.
1 cup (8 ounces) low-fat coffee yogurt	
2 tablespoons chocolate syrup	*Cover* jar with lid. Press POWER, then press SMOOTHIE. Press START/STOP.
6 ice cubes	*Pour* into tall glass to serve.

Oster

Entertaining Tip

This recipe is easily doubled to share with someone in the morning. It's a great way to start the day and also makes a tasty, low-fat treat for dessert.

cranberry orange pumpkin scones
with whipped maple butter

MAKES 8 SCONES

2 cups all-purpose flour

⅓ cup packed brown sugar

¼ teaspoon finely chopped crystallized ginger

¼ teaspoon ground nutmeg

½ teaspoon ground cinnamon

1 teaspoon grated orange peel

1 teaspoon baking powder

¼ teaspoon baking soda

¼ teaspoon salt

½ cup (1 stick) cold unsalted butter, cut into pieces

⅓ cup buttermilk

½ cup fresh or canned puréed pumpkin (not pumpkin pie filling)

1 teaspoon pure orange extract

½ cup dried cranberries

½ cup chopped pecans (optional)

1 egg

1 teaspoon water

Turbinado sugar (optional)

Whipped Maple Butter (recipe follows)

Preheat oven to 400°F. Line baking sheet with parchment paper.

Combine first 9 ingredients in large bowl and mix with Oster® Hand Mixer, being sure to crumble any lumps of brown sugar. Add cold butter and beat mixture until it comes together into coarse crumbs.

Stir buttermilk, pumpkin purée and orange extract together in separate bowl. Add buttermilk mixture, cranberries and pecans, if desired, to flour mixture and stir just until dough comes together. Do not overmix.

Turn dough out onto prepared baking sheet and pat dough into circle about 7 inches across and 1½ inches thick.

Beat egg and water together until well combined. Brush top of dough with egg wash and sprinkle with turbinado sugar, if desired. Score dough into 8 equal wedges.

Bake about 20 minutes or until golden and toothpick inserted in middle comes out clean. Remove from oven and cool on wire rack. Separate scones and serve warm or at room temperature with Whipped Maple Butter.

whipped maple butter

1 cup (2 sticks) unsalted butter, softened	*Combine* all ingredients in small bowl. Attach whisks to Oster® Hand Mixer and whip until light, fluffy and well blended. Use immediately, or refrigerate in airtight container up to 2 weeks or freeze up to 3 months.
1 tablespoon powdered sugar	
2 tablespoons maple syrup (not maple-flavored breakfast syrup)	*MAKES 1 CUP*

triple blueberry waffles

MAKES 6 SERVINGS

2 cups milk, divided
½ teaspoon active dry yeast
1 cup all-purpose flour
1 cup bread flour
½ teaspoon salt
1 tablespoon blueberry preserves
½ cup (1 stick) unsalted butter, melted and cooled
1 teaspoon vanilla
¾ cup dried blueberries
4 to 5 ounces fresh blueberries
2 eggs

Eight hours before serving or before going to bed, gently warm ½ cup milk to about 105° to 110°F. Stir yeast into milk and set aside 5 minutes.

Combine dry ingredients and stir in yeast mixture, remaining milk, preserves, butter and vanilla. Batter will be loose. Cover with plastic wrap and refrigerate 8 hours or overnight.

Place dried blueberries in separate small bowl and cover with water. Cover with plastic wrap and refrigerate 8 hours or overnight.

Preheat Oster® Wafflemaker to next-to-highest setting when ready to prepare waffles.

Remove batter and blueberries from refrigerator. Drain liquid from soaked blueberries.

Separate eggs. Stir yolks, soaked dried blueberries and fresh blueberries into batter. Beat whites to soft peaks and gently fold into batter.

Cook waffles 8 minutes or to desired doneness.

breakfast rice pudding

MAKES 4 (½-CUP) SERVINGS

1½ cups milk

½ cup instant brown rice

¼ cup rolled oats

⅓ cup packed light brown sugar

½ teaspoon ground cinnamon

⅛ teaspoon salt

½ cup half-and-half or milk, or more to taste, divided

¼ cup golden raisins (optional)

½ teaspoon vanilla

⅛ teaspoon almond extract

Fresh or frozen mixed berries, partially thawed (optional)

In medium saucepan over medium-high heat, bring milk just to a boil. Stir in rice, oats, sugar, cinnamon and salt. Return just to a boil, reduce heat, cover tightly and simmer 10 minutes.

Stir in ½ cup half-and-half. Add raisins, if desired. Cover tightly; simmer 10 minutes more. Remove from heat. Stir in vanilla and almond extract. (Pudding thickens as it cools. For a thinner consistency, add ¼ cup more half-and-half, if desired.) Serve as-is or topped with berries, if desired.

Oster.

Entertaining Tip

Want to jazz up breakfast? Allow pudding to cool slightly before serving in a heat-safe martini glass.

honey granola with yogurt

MAKES 6 SERVINGS

½ cup uncooked old-fashioned oats
¼ cup sliced almonds
2 tablespoons wheat germ, toasted
1 tablespoon orange juice
1 tablespoon honey
½ teaspoon ground cinnamon
1 ½ cups whole strawberries
4 containers (6 ounces each) plain yogurt
1 teaspoon vanilla
Fresh mint sprigs (optional)

Preheat oven to 350°F. Lightly spray 8-inch square baking pan with nonstick cooking spray; set aside.

Combine oats, almonds and wheat germ in small bowl. Combine orange juice, honey and cinnamon in another small bowl. Add juice mixture to oat mixture; mix well. Spread mixture evenly in prepared pan.

Bake 20 to 25 minutes or until toasted, stirring twice during baking. Spread mixture on large sheet of foil; cool completely.

Cut 3 strawberries in half for garnish. Slice remaining strawberries. Combine yogurt and vanilla in medium bowl. Layer yogurt mixture, granola and sliced strawberries in 6 dessert dishes. Garnish with strawberry halves and mint sprigs.

Oster®

Entertaining Tip

This recipe is ideal for a summer brunch with friends. Bake the granola fresh in your Oster® Countertop Oven and you won't heat up the kitchen before your guests arrive.

ham & egg breakfast panini

MAKES 2 SANDWICHES

Nonstick cooking spray

¼ cup chopped green or red bell pepper

2 tablespoons sliced green onions

1 slice (1 ounce) reduced-fat smoked deli ham, chopped (¼ cup)

½ cup cholesterol-free egg substitute

Black pepper

4 slices multigrain or whole grain bread

2 (¾-ounce) slices reduced-fat Cheddar cheese or Swiss cheese

Spray small skillet with cooking spray; heat over medium heat. Add bell pepper and green onions; cook and stir 4 minutes or until vegetables begin to soften. Add ham.

Combine egg substitute and black pepper in small bowl; pour into skillet. Cook about 2 minutes, stirring occasionally until egg mixture is almost set. Remove from heat.

Heat grill pan over medium heat until hot. Spray 1 side of each bread slice with cooking spray; turn bread over. Top each of 2 bread slices with 1 slice cheese and half of egg mixture. Top with remaining bread slices.

Grill sandwiches about 2 minutes per side, pressing sandwiches lightly with spatula, until toasted. (If desired, cover pan with lid during last 2 minutes of cooking to melt cheese.) Cut sandwiches in half and serve immediately.

Oster

Entertaining Tip

For even easier preparation, toast assembled panini in an Oster® Wafflemaker fitted with sandwich plates.

phyllo breakfast spirals

MAKES 8 SERVINGS (ABOUT 3 SLICES PER SERVING)

½ cup (1 stick) butter, melted, divided

¼ cup finely chopped onion

2 teaspoons minced garlic

9 eggs, well beaten

½ teaspoon black pepper

¼ teaspoon salt

½ cup finely chopped red bell pepper

⅓ cup crumbled feta *or* shredded pepper jack cheese

16 pitted kalamata olives, coarsely chopped *or* 3 ounces Canadian bacon, finely chopped

1½ tablespoons chopped fresh oregano *or* chopped fresh cilantro

20 sheets frozen phyllo dough, thawed (about half of 16-ounce package)

1 egg

1 tablespoon water

Preheat oven to 350°F. Line large baking sheet with parchment paper.

Heat 1 tablespoon butter in large nonstick skillet over medium heat. Add onion and garlic; cook and stir 2 to 3 minutes or until onion is translucent. Add beaten eggs, black pepper and salt; cook until eggs are almost set, stirring frequently. Add bell pepper, feta, olives and oregano; stir until just blended. Remove from heat and set aside to cool slightly.

Place sheet of parchment paper on clean work surface. Place 1 sheet phyllo on parchment; brush with melted butter and top with second sheet of phyllo. Repeat layers of phyllo sheets and butter until 10 sheets are stacked. Spoon half of egg mixture along 1 long side of phyllo stack. Starting with egg side, roll up jelly-roll style, tucking in sides. Carefully transfer roll to prepared baking sheet, placing seam side down. Repeat to make second roll. Whisk remaining egg and water in small bowl until well blended; brush evenly over rolls.

Bake 18 minutes or until golden. Cool on baking sheet on wire rack 10 minutes before cutting into 1-inch slices with serrated knife.

Note: Rolls may be assembled, covered with plastic wrap and refrigerated up to 24 hours in advance. Bake 3 minutes longer than directed above or until golden.

smoked salmon hash browns

MAKES 4 SERVINGS

3	**cups frozen hash brown potatoes, thawed**
2	**pouches (3 ounces each) smoked salmon***
½	**cup chopped onion**
½	**cup chopped bell pepper**
¼	**teaspoon black pepper**
2	**tablespoons vegetable oil**

*Smoked salmon in foil packages can be found in the canned fish section of the supermarket. Do not substitute lox or other fresh smoked salmon.

Combine potatoes, salmon, onion, bell pepper and black pepper in large bowl; mix well.

Heat oil in large nonstick skillet over medium-high heat. Add potato mixture; spread to cover surface of skillet. Carefully pat down to avoid oil spatter.

Cook 5 minutes or until crisp and browned. Turn over in large pieces. Cook 2 to 3 minutes or until brown.

light 'n' crisp waffles

MAKES 8 SERVINGS

2	egg yolks
½	teaspoon salt
2	cups milk
½	cup vegetable oil
2	cups all-purpose flour
1	tablespoon baking powder
2	egg whites, stiffly beaten

Preheat Oster® Wafflemaker.

Combine all ingredients except egg whites in large bowl. Mix with electric mixer on low until moistened. Increase to medium speed and beat until smooth. Fold in beaten egg whites by hand.

Pour ½ cup batter over wafflemaker grids. Close and bake until steam no longer escapes, about 3 to 5 minutes. Repeat with remaining batter.

Variations: Challenge your creativity in the kitchen with the Oster® Wafflemaker. Whatever your preferred variety, you'll love these crisp waffles made with egg whites, milk and all-purpose flour. Try some of these sweet or savory variations:

Pecan or Macadamia Nut Waffles: Sprinkle 1 tablespoon finely chopped pecans or macadamia nuts over preheated waffle grids. Pour ½ cup batter over nuts and close wafflemaker. Bake as directed.

Bacon Waffles: Cook 8 bacon strips to desired doneness. Pour ½ cup batter over waffle grids. Crumble 1 strip bacon, sprinkle over batter and close wafflemaker. Bake as directed.

Cheese Waffles: Fold 1½ cups shredded Cheddar cheese into batter. Bake as directed.

Blueberry Waffles: Fold 2 cups fresh blueberries into batter. Pour ¾ cup batter over grids. Bake until golden.

Chocolate Chip Waffles: Fold 1 cup chocolate chips into batter. Bake as directed.

cinnamon-nut bubble ring

MAKES 12 SERVINGS

DOUGH

¾	cup apple juice, at room temperature
1	egg
2	tablespoons butter, softened
1	teaspoon salt
3	cups bread flour
½	cup finely chopped walnuts
¼	cup granulated sugar
2	tablespoons nonfat dry milk powder
¼	teaspoon ground cinnamon
2	teaspoons active dry yeast

CINNAMON COATING

½	cup granulated sugar
4	teaspoons ground cinnamon
3	tablespoons butter, melted

APPLE GLAZE

1	cup powdered sugar
4	to 5 teaspoons apple juice

Measuring carefully, place all dough ingredients in Oster® Bread Machine pan in order specified. Select DOUGH setting; press start. (Do not use delay cycle.) Lightly grease 10-inch tube pan; set aside.

When cycle is complete, remove dough to lightly floured surface. If necessary, knead in additional bread flour to make dough easy to handle. Combine granulated sugar and cinnamon in shallow bowl to make Cinnamon Coating; pour melted butter into small bowl. Shape dough into 2-inch balls. Roll in melted butter; coat evenly with Cinnamon Coating mixture. Place in prepared pan. Cover with clean towel; let rise in warm, draft-free place 1 to 1½ hours or until doubled in size.

Preheat oven to 350°F. Bake bread 30 minutes or until golden brown. Let cool in pan on wire rack 10 minutes; carefully remove from pan. Cool completely.

For Apple Glaze, combine powdered sugar and apple juice in medium bowl until smooth; drizzle over bubble ring.

Note: To warm apple juice, place in 2-cup microwavable glass measuring cup and heat on HIGH 10 to 15 seconds or to desired temperature.

bratwurst skillet breakfast

MAKES 4 SERVINGS

1½	**pounds red potatoes**
3	**bratwurst links (about ¾ pound)**
2	**tablespoons butter or margarine**
1½	**teaspoons caraway seeds**
4	**cups shredded red cabbage**

Cut potatoes into ¼- to ½-inch pieces. Place in microwavable baking dish. Microwave, covered, on HIGH 3 minutes; stir. Microwave 2 minutes more or until just tender; set aside.

Meanwhile, cut bratwurst into ¼-inch slices. Cook bratwurst in large skillet over medium-high heat 8 minutes or until browned and no longer pink in center. Remove from pan with slotted spoon; set aside. Pour off drippings.

Melt butter in same skillet. Add potatoes and caraway seeds. Cook, stirring occasionally, 6 to 8 minutes or until potatoes are golden and tender. Return sausage to skillet; stir in cabbage. Cook, covered, 3 minutes or until cabbage is slightly wilted. Uncover and stir 3 to 4 minutes more or until cabbage is just tender yet still bright red.

Stylish at Sunup

honey-wheat pancakes

MAKES ABOUT 16 PANCAKES

Beat buttermilk, eggs and honey together until well combined.

Stir together baking mix, flour, wheat germ and baking powder in a separate bowl. Pour buttermilk mixture into flour mixture and stir just until combined.

Pour ¼ cupfuls of batter onto preheated Oster® Electric Skillet. Cook until tops begin to bubble, turn over and continue to cook until golden. Serve hot with butter and syrup.

1⅓	cups low-fat buttermilk
2	eggs
2	tablespoons honey
1½	cups reduced-fat buttermilk baking mix
½	cup whole wheat flour
¼	cup honey-crunch wheat germ
1	teaspoon baking powder
	Butter and syrup

Oster

Entertaining Tip

Simplify your mornings with the power of the Oster® Blender. Just place the ingredients (in the order given above) into a blender jar. Your pancake batter will be ready in no time.

easy raspberry-peach danish

MAKES 32 SERVINGS (2 THIN SLICES PER SERVING)

1 loaf (16 ounces) frozen white bread dough, thawed

⅓ cup raspberry fruit spread

1 can (16 ounces) sliced peaches in juice, drained and chopped

Egg white (optional)

2 to 3 teaspoons orange juice

½ cup powdered sugar

¼ cup chopped pecans, toasted

Preheat oven to 350°F. Spray 2 baking sheets with nonstick cooking spray.

Place dough on lightly floured surface. Cut dough in half. Roll each half into 12×7-inch rectangle. Place 1 rectangle on each prepared baking sheet.

Spread half of raspberry spread over center third of each dough rectangle. Sprinkle peaches over raspberry spread. Make 2-inch cuts every inch along both long sides of each Danish. Starting at one end, alternately fold opposite strips of dough over filling.

Cover; let rise in warm place about 1 hour or until nearly doubled in size. Bake 15 to 20 minutes or until golden. If deeper golden color is desired, lightly brush egg white over tops of loaves during last 5 minutes of baking. Remove baked loaves from baking sheet. Cool slightly.

Stir just enough orange juice into powdered sugar in small bowl to form smooth glaze. Drizzle over both loaves and sprinkle with pecans.

ham-egg-brie strudel

MAKES 4 SERVINGS

4	**eggs**
1	**tablespoon minced green onion**
1	**tablespoon minced parsley**
¼	**teaspoon salt**
⅛	**teaspoon black pepper**
1	**tablespoon vegetable oil**
4	**sheets phyllo pastry**
2	**tablespoons butter or margarine, melted**
3	**ounces sliced ham**
3	**ounces Brie cheese**

Preheat oven to 375°F. Lightly beat eggs; add green onion, parsley, salt and pepper. Heat oil in medium skillet over medium-low heat. Add egg mixture; cook and stir until softly scrambled. Set aside.

Place 1 phyllo sheet on large piece of waxed paper. Brush lightly with butter. Top with second phyllo sheet; brush with butter. Repeat with remaining phyllo sheets. Arrange half of ham slices along short end of pastry, leaving 2-inch border around short end and sides. Place scrambled eggs over ham. Cut cheese into small pieces. Place over eggs; top with remaining ham.

Fold in long sides of phyllo; fold short end over ham. Use waxed paper to roll pastry to enclose filling. Place on lightly greased baking sheet, seam-side down. Brush with remaining butter. Bake about 15 minutes or until lightly browned. Slice and serve immediately.

eggs benedict
with asparagus & crab

MAKES 2 SERVINGS

Combine parsley and oil in Oster® Blender or Oster® Food Processor and process until blended. Transfer to airtight container and reserve for later use.

Bring 2 inches of water and vinegar to a boil in large Oster® Skillet over medium-high heat. Reduce heat and simmer water. Crack 1 egg into shallow dish. Pour egg from dish into water in one quick motion. Repeat quickly with remaining eggs. Poach eggs 4 to 5 minutes until white is firm and opaque but yolk remains liquid. Remove eggs with a slotted spoon and drain on paper towels.

Meanwhile, split English muffins and toast in Oster® Toaster until golden brown.

To serve, place 2 muffin halves on each of 2 plates. Top each with 1 slice bacon, poached egg and 1 crab claw. Top each with one fourth of Hollandaise Sauce, and garnish with parsley oil. Serve with steamed asparagus.

¼ cup lightly packed fresh parsley sprigs
¼ cup vegetable oil
1 teaspoon vinegar
4 eggs
2 English muffins
4 thin slices Canadian bacon, fried until golden and kept warm
4 whole crab claws, cooked and kept warm
Hollandaise Sauce (recipe follows)
Steamed asparagus, kept warm

hollandaise sauce

Place egg yolks, water and lemon juice in blender. Blend 1 minute.

With blender running, pour butter through open hole of blender lid.

Season with salt and pepper and keep warm.

MAKES ABOUT 1 CUP

3 egg yolks
1 tablespoon hot water
1 tablespoon lemon juice
½ cup (1 stick) unsalted butter, melted and hot
Salt and pepper

Sophisticated Entertaining

goat cheese stuffed figs

MAKES 4 TO 6 SERVINGS

7	fresh firm, ripe figs
7	slices prosciutto
1	package (4 ounces) goat cheese
	Black pepper

Preheat broiler. Line small baking sheet or broiler pan with foil. Cut figs in half vertically. Cut prosciutto slices in half to create 14 pieces (about 4 inches long and 1 inch wide).

Scoop 1 teaspoon goat cheese onto cut side of each fig half. Wrap prosciutto slice around fig and goat cheese. Sprinkle with pepper.

Broil about 4 minutes or until cheese softens and until figs are heated through.

Oster

Entertaining Tip

Fresh figs are extremely perishable and should be used soon after purchase. Store them unwashed in the refrigerator for 2 or 3 days.

wine biscuits

MAKES ABOUT 6½ DOZEN BISCUITS

¼ cup sugar
3 cups all-purpose unbleached flour
1½ cups semolina flour
1 tablespoon plus 1 teaspoon baking powder
1 to 2 tablespoons black pepper (or to taste)
1 cup dry Burgundy table wine
1 cup vegetable oil
¼ cup grated Parmesan cheese
2 to 3 tablespoons finely chopped fresh rosemary or lavender
1 egg, lightly beaten
1 tablespoon water

Preheat oven to 350°F.

Add sugar, flours, baking powder and pepper to food processor bowl. Turn food processor on and pour wine and oil through feeding tube while processing. Dough will form 1 big ball. (Or you may put all dry ingredients in large bowl and work in wet ingredients by hand.)

Remove dough and divide into 3 equal portions.

Knead cheese into 1 portion, rosemary into second portion, but leave third portion as-is.

Roll out each portion of dough to ¼-inch thickness, and cut shapes with cookie or biscuit cutter.*

Beat egg and water together. Brush on tops of biscuits. Bake biscuits on cookie sheets about 20 minutes or until slightly golden. Remove biscuits from oven and cool completely on wire racks.

Oster

*Traditionally these biscuits are cut into teaspoon-sized balls and rolled pencil thin, then the ends are joined to form a circle. They are baked twice to make them crispy.

Entertaining Tip

Host a wine and cheese party! Have your guests bring a bottle of their favorite wine. Using your Oster® Wine Opener is effortless and allows you to spend more time with your guests.

chorizo & artichoke kabobs
with mustard vinaigrette

MAKES 6 SERVINGS

1 can (14 ounces) large artichoke hearts, well drained

2 (3-ounce) chorizo-flavored chicken sausages or andouille sausages, fully cooked

3 tablespoons olive oil

2 teaspoons white wine vinegar

1 teaspoon Dijon-style mustard

1/16 teaspoon salt

1/16 teaspoon black pepper

Preheat broiler. Line baking sheet or broiler pan with heavy-duty foil.

Cut artichoke hearts in half. Cut each sausage diagonally into 6 slices. Arrange 2 artichoke pieces and 2 sausage slices on each of 6 wooden skewers. (Soak wooden skewers in warm water 20 minutes before using.) Arrange skewers on baking sheet. Broil 4 inches from heat 4 minutes or until artichokes are hot and sausage is browned.

For vinaigrette, combine oil, vinegar, mustard, salt and pepper in small bowl. Serve with kabobs.

jumbo lump crabmeat
with potato pancakes, mango and baby greens

MAKES 4 SERVINGS

3	large Idaho potatoes, peeled and shredded
¾	cup finely diced onion
1	egg
½	teaspoon baking soda
1	tablespoon all-purpose flour
	Salt and black pepper
4	tablespoons blended oil (canola and vegetable), divided
1	cup finely sliced shallots
⅔	cup brandy
2	cups heavy cream
1	pound fresh jumbo lump crabmeat
1	mango, peeled and diced (dice 1 teaspoon finely and reserve for vinaigrette)
2	cups baby greens
	Mango Vinaigrette (recipe follows)

Chop potato and onion in Oster® Food Processor and transfer to large bowl. Add egg and baking soda. Add flour in small amounts to bind mixture. Season with salt and pepper to taste.

Heat 2 tablespoons oil in Oster® Electric Skillet. Spoon potato mixture on skillet surface to make silver-dollar pancakes. When pancake begins to dry out at edges, turn over. Make at least 12 pancakes (this recipe will yield 20).

Heat remaining 2 tablespoons oil in Oster® Electric Skillet over medium heat. Add shallots; cook and stir until they begin to caramelize.

Add brandy and carefully ignite using barbecue pit lighter; let flame until brandy burns out. Stir in cream and bring to a boil. Reduce heat to simmer. Reduce cream by half. Turn off heat; add salt and pepper.

Reheat potato pancakes in 350°F Oster® Countertop Oven. Meanwhile, stir crabmeat into brandy cream. Heat gently, stirring to coat crabmeat. Taste and adjust seasonings.

Place diced mango on plates and drizzle with Mango Vinaigrette. Mix some Mango Vinaigrette with greens. Place greens on plates. Scoop some crab-cream mixture over each potato pancake.

mango vinaigrette

Whisk first 5 ingredients together; do not use blender. Season to taste with salt and pepper.

1	**tablespoon mango syrup or nectar**
¼	**teaspoon minced jalapeño pepper**
1	**tablespoon champagne vinegar**
1	**teaspoon finely diced mango**
½	**cup blended oil (canola and vegetable)**
	Salt and black pepper

moroccan chicken turnovers

MAKES 8 TURNOVERS

½	**cup (1 stick) plus 2 tablespoons butter, divided**
⅔	**cup finely chopped onions**
½	**cup finely chopped carrots**
1½	**teaspoons grated fresh ginger**
½	**teaspoon salt**
½	**teaspoon dried oregano**
½	**teaspoon ground cumin**
¼	**teaspoon paprika**
⅛	**teaspoon ground red pepper**
⅓	**cup water**
¼	**cup tomato paste**
2	**cups finely chopped cooked chicken**
16	**sheets frozen phyllo dough, thawed**

Melt 2 tablespoons butter in medium skillet over medium heat. Add onions and carrots; cook 6 to 8 minutes or until very soft, stirring frequently. Add ginger, salt, oregano, cumin, paprika and red pepper; cook and stir 1 minute. Stir in water and tomato paste until well blended. Add chicken; cook and stir 2 minutes. (Mixture will be very thick.) Spread filling in shallow pan; place in freezer 15 minutes to cool. (Filling may be prepared up to 24 hours in advance; store covered in refrigerator.)

Preheat oven to 350°F. Melt remaining ½ cup butter. Stack 4 sheets phyllo on work surface or cutting board, brushing each with melted butter before adding next sheet. Cut phyllo stack in half lengthwise.

Place ¼ cup cooled filling about 1 inch from bottom of each strip. Fold one corner of phyllo diagonally across to opposite edge to form triangle; continue to fold triangle up as you would fold a flag. Arrange triangles seam side down, at least 1 inch apart, on ungreased baking sheet; brush tops with melted butter. Repeat with remaining phyllo, chicken filling and melted butter.

Bake 20 to 22 minutes or until golden.

Oster

Entertaining Tip

To make smaller appetizer turnovers instead of entrées, cut each stack of phyllo crosswise into 4 strips and use 1 to 2 tablespoons filling for each triangle. Brush with butter and fold up triangles as directed above. Bake at 350°F about 15 minutes.

mini gingerbread wheat cakes

MAKES 6 SERVINGS

¾ cup whole wheat flour
½ cup all-purpose flour
1 tablespoon ground ginger
1½ teaspoons baking powder
1 teaspoon cinnamon
1 teaspoon grated orange peel
½ teaspoon salt
¼ teaspoon baking soda
¼ teaspoon ground cloves
¼ teaspoon ground nutmeg
¼ cup (½ stick) butter, softened
¼ cup granulated sugar
¼ cup packed brown sugar
1 egg
½ cup dark molasses
½ cup hot water
Whipped cream
Fresh mint sprigs (optional)

Preheat oven to 350°F. Grease 6 (4-inch) miniature bundt pans very well with shortening. Dust cups lightly with flour. Set aside.

Combine flours, ginger, baking powder, cinnamon, orange peel, salt, baking soda, cloves and nutmeg in small bowl; set aside.

Place butter, sugars and egg in large bowl; beat with electric mixer at medium speed until light and fluffy. Add molasses; beat well. Add flour mixture alternately with water. Beat on low speed just until blended. Evenly divide batter among prepared pans.

Bake 20 to 25 minutes or until toothpick inserted near centers comes out clean. Cool in pans 10 minutes. Carefully run edge of knife around inside and outside edge of pans. Invert on wire rack; cool completely. Serve with whipped cream and garnish with mint sprigs, if desired.

Sophisticated Entertaining

lemon chicken
with moroccan olives, pine nuts, toasted garlic & couscous

MAKES 4 SERVINGS

½ cup plus 2 tablespoons olive oil, divided

2 lemons, juiced and chopped (use Moroccan preserved lemons, if available)

1½ tablespoons roughly chopped cilantro leaves, divided

1 tablespoon plus 2 teaspoons minced fresh ginger, divided

Pinch red pepper flakes

1 teaspoon white pepper

2 chickens (3 pounds each)

Salt and black pepper

5 tablespoons grated white onion

1 teaspoon minced garlic

Pinch saffron

⅓ cup sliced Moroccan green olives

⅓ cup pine nuts, toasted

3 tablespoons lemon juice

3 tablespoons honey

1 quart chicken stock, reduced to 2 cups

2 tablespoons butter

1 teaspoon chopped fresh parsley

Couscous (recipe follows)

Combine ½ cup olive oil, lemons, ½ tablespoon cilantro, 2 teaspoons ginger, red pepper flakes and white pepper. Place chickens in food storage bag with marinade. Turn to coat; refrigerate 6 to 24 hours.

Preheat oven to 375°F.

Remove chickens from marinade, season with salt and pepper inside and out and truss. Heat remaining 2 tablespoons olive oil in ovenproof roasting pan over high heat. Brown chickens in oil until golden on all sides. Roast chickens 50 minutes. Remove chickens from roasting pan and set aside.

Reserve 3 tablespoons drippings in pan; discard remaining drippings. Add onion, remaining 1 tablespoon ginger and garlic. Cook over medium heat until onion begins to brown. Add crushed red pepper to taste, saffron, olives and pine nuts.

Add lemon juice to pan, stirring to scrape up browned bits. Add honey and chicken stock; cook until reduced by half. Stir in butter, parsley and remaining 1 tablespoon cilantro. Add salt and pepper to taste. Reserve and keep warm.

Brown chickens further under broiler if necessary. Remove trussing and carve. Drizzle sauce over chicken and garnish with chopped chives or cilantro leaves. Serve with Couscous.

COUSCOUS

Bring chicken stock to a simmer.

Heat oil in large sauté pan over medium heat. Add carrot, red pepper, onion and zucchini. Cook and stir until tender. Add saffron, turmeric and stock.

Place dry couscous in large bowl; add vegetable mixture. Stir to combine.

Cover with plastic wrap and let steam approximately 15 minutes. Add parsley and fluff with fork before serving.

2	**cups chicken stock**
1	**tablespoon olive oil**
1	**medium carrot, cut into ¼-inch cubes**
½	**red bell pepper, seeded and diced**
½	**onion, diced**
½	**zucchini, diced**
	Pinch saffron
1	**tablespoon ground turmeric**
2	**cups medium-grain couscous**
4	**tablespoons chopped fresh parsley**

chocolate hazelnut cupcakes

MAKES 18 CUPCAKES

1¾	cups all-purpose flour
1½	teaspoons baking powder
½	teaspoon salt
2	cups chocolate hazelnut spread, divided
⅓	cup butter, softened
¾	cup sugar
2	eggs
1	teaspoon vanilla
1¼	cups milk
	Chopped hazelnuts (optional)

Preheat oven to 350°F. Line 18 standard (2½-inch) muffin cups with paper or foil baking cups.

Combine flour, baking powder and salt in medium bowl. Beat ⅓ cup chocolate hazelnut spread and butter in large bowl with electric mixer at medium speed until smooth. Beat in sugar until well blended. Beat in eggs and vanilla. Add flour mixture alternately with milk, beginning and ending with flour mixture. Spoon batter into prepared muffin cups, filling two-thirds full.

Bake 20 to 23 minutes or until cupcakes spring back when touched and toothpick inserted into centers comes out clean. Cool cupcakes in pans 10 minutes. Remove from pans; cool completely on wire racks.

Frost tops of cupcakes with remaining chocolate hazelnut spread. Sprinkle with hazelnuts.

mesquite-grilled tiger prawns
with pesto, cannellini beans, grilled radicchio, fennel and confit tomatoes

MAKES 4 SERVINGS

2	fennel bulbs, trimmed
1	head radicchio
	Salt and white pepper
3	tablespoons olive oil, divided
16	tiger prawns, shelled
	Pesto Sauce (recipe follows)
4	(8-inch) wooden skewers
2	cups chopped hearts of romaine
2	cups arugula leaves
½	cup fresh basil leaves
½	cup Confit Tomatoes (recipe follows)
1	tablespoon lemon juice
2	cups cannellini beans, cooked with garlic and rosemary

Cut fennel bulbs into ¼-inch wedges and cut radicchio into 8 wedges. Season to taste with salt and pepper. Drizzle with 1 tablespoon olive oil. Grill over mesquite coals until fennel is golden brown and soft and radicchio is lightly colored and wilted. Refrigerate until serving.

Skewer 4 prawns on each skewer. Brush with Pesto Sauce and grill over mesquite coals until opaque.

Toss romaine, arugula and basil leaves with Confit Tomatoes, lemon juice and remaining 2 tablespoons olive oil. Place a mound of greens in centers of 4 serving plates.

Combine cannellini beans with chilled fennel-radicchio mixture. Spoon mixture over greens. Top each plate with a shrimp skewer and drizzle with Pesto Sauce.

pesto sauce

Combine all ingredients in Oster® Blender. Purée until smooth.

1	cup fresh basil leaves
2	tablespoons chopped pine nuts
1	tablespoon chopped garlic
2	tablespoons grated Parmesan cheese
½	cup olive oil

confit tomatoes

Preheat oven to 300°F. Combine tomatoes and olive oil on baking pan; season to taste with salt and pepper. Crush garlic cloves and scatter around tomatoes. Add thyme.

Bake approximately 45 minutes or until tomatoes have cooked down to a quarter of their size. Remove from oven and cool to room temperature.

When cool, remove tomatoes from oil and serve. Strain oil and reserve for another use. Roasted garlic and thyme can be used in stocks. This recipe makes more than needed for above recipe.

MAKES ABOUT 1 CUP TOMATOES AND 2 CUPS FLAVORED OIL

10	Roma tomatoes, peeled, seeded and chopped
2	cups extra-virgin olive oil
	Salt and ground white pepper
2	heads garlic, broken into cloves and left unpeeled
1	bunch fresh thyme

almond-coated scallops

MAKES 4 SERVINGS

2	**tablespoons plus 1½ teaspoons olive oil, divided**
1	**clove garlic, crushed**
¼	**cup coarse plain dry bread crumbs**
2	**tablespoons sliced almonds, chopped**
1½	**teaspoons grated lemon peel, divided**
¼	**teaspoon salt**
	Black pepper
8	**jumbo sea scallops, cut in half horizontally (about 1 pound)**

Heat 2 tablespoons oil in medium skillet over low heat. Add garlic; cook and stir 2 minutes. Remove from heat. Discard garlic.

Combine bread crumbs, almonds, 1 teaspoon lemon peel and salt on plate; season with pepper. Brush scallop slices with remaining 1½ teaspoons oil. Press scallops into bread crumb mixture to coat both sides.

Reheat oil in skillet over medium-high heat. Cook scallops in batches 2 to 3 minutes or until golden. Turn and cook 1 to 2 minutes. Sprinkle with remaining ½ teaspoon lemon peel. Serve immediately.

shrimp and scallop tapas

MAKES 12 SERVINGS

Pat scallops dry. Cut small pocket in each of 12 scallops with tip of paring knife. Spoon about 1 teaspoon pesto sauce into each pocket. Wrap 1 slice bacon around each scallop, fully covering pesto-filled pocket, and secure with toothpick.

Slit shrimp lengthwise, leaving tail on. Wrap each shrimp around one of the remaining 12 scallops and secure with toothpicks.

Place 6 scallops at a time on Oster® Quesadilla Maker and cook 5 to 8 minutes or until done. Repeat with remaining scallops. Serve 1 pesto-filled scallop and 1 shrimp-wrapped scallop to each person.

24	large sea scallops
½	cup prepared pesto sauce
1	package fully-cooked bacon slices
12	large shrimp

citrus-marinated atlantic salmon
with potato blinis and garden greens

MAKES 4 SERVINGS

MARINATED SALMON

1	salmon fillet (2 pounds)
1½	cups kosher salt, divided
¼	teaspoon white pepper, divided
½	cup sugar, divided
1½	teaspoons grated lemon peel
1½	teaspoons grated orange peel
1½	teaspoons grated lime peel
1½	teaspoons grated grapefruit peel

POTATO BLINIS

1	pound russet potatoes, peeled
3	tablespoons milk
3	tablespoons all-purpose flour
3	eggs
3	tablespoons crème fraîche or heavy cream
3	egg whites
	Salt and white pepper
1	cup greens, washed and dried
	Citrus Vinaigrette (recipe follows)

Line sheet pan with piece of aluminum foil large enough to envelop salmon. Place half of salt, pepper and sugar on foil. Place salmon on salt mixture, skin side down.

Rub flesh side with citrus zests and remaining salt, pepper and sugar. Fold aluminum foil over and place another sheet pan, weighted, directly on top of salmon.

Place in refrigerator. (This will help extract liquid and compact flesh). Let marinate at least 24 hours (can be kept up to 1 week). Remove salmon from marinade and rinse under cold water. Pat dry.

Cover potatoes with water in large saucepan. Bring to a boil over high heat. Reduce heat to low and simmer 20 minutes or until tender. Drain. Pass potatoes through ricer. Add milk and flour and mix with Oster® Hand Mixer.

Add remaining ingredients, beating after each addition. Season with salt and pepper.

Heat Oster® Electric Skillet to 325°F. Spoon blini mixture about 1 tablespoon at a time onto griddle, and cook as for pancakes. This should be done at the last minute to insure that blinis stay warm.

Place warm blinis in center of each plate. Top with 3 slices marinated salmon. Dress greens with Citrus Vinaigrette and place on top of salmon. Serve immediately.

citrus vinaigrette

Whisk all ingredients together with Oster® Hand Mixer. (This recipe makes more than enough. Store in container that permits shaking to mix ingredients before serving.)

¼	cup lemon juice
¼	cup lime juice
¼	cup grapefruit juice
¼	cup orange juice
2	tablespoons white wine vinegar
½	cup extra-virgin olive oil

shrimp, goat cheese & leek tortilla

MAKES 6 TO 8 SERVINGS

8 ounces medium raw shrimp, peeled and deveined
4 tablespoons olive oil, divided
2 cloves garlic, minced
2 leeks, chopped
7 eggs
Salt and black pepper
1 package (3 ounces) goat cheese

Preheat oven to 350°F. Cut each shrimp into 4 pieces.

Heat 2 tablespoons oil in medium skillet with ovenproof handle over medium-high heat. Add garlic; cook and stir 30 seconds or just until fragrant. Add shrimp; cook and stir 3 to 4 minutes or until shrimp are pink and opaque. Remove to plate; set aside.

Heat remaining 2 tablespoons oil in same skillet over medium heat. Add leeks; cook and stir 4 to 5 minutes or until tender. Remove to plate with shrimp; cool 5 minutes.

Whisk eggs in medium bowl; season with salt and pepper. Crumble goat cheese into eggs. Stir in shrimp and leeks.

Spray same skillet with nonstick cooking spray; heat over medium-low heat. Add egg mixture; cook 5 minutes or until edges begin to set. Transfer skillet to oven; bake 10 to 12 minutes or until surface is puffy and center is just set. Remove; cool 10 minutes. Cut into wedges; serve warm or at room temperature.

Family
Celebrations

fresh spinach-strawberry salad

MAKES 5 (2-CUP) SERVINGS

2 to 4 ounces slivered almonds	
1 bag (9 ounces) spinach leaves	
¾ cup thinly sliced red onion	
⅓ cup pomegranate or pomegranate-cherry juice	
2 tablespoons toasted (dark) sesame oil	
2 tablespoons vegetable oil	
3 tablespoons cider vinegar	
3 tablespoons sugar	
¼ teaspoon red pepper flakes	
⅛ teaspoon salt	
2 cups quartered strawberries	
4 ounces goat cheese, crumbled or sliced (optional)	

Place medium skillet over medium heat until hot. Add almonds; cook 2 minutes or until beginning to lightly brown, stirring constantly. Remove to plate; set aside to cool.

Meanwhile, combine spinach and onion in large serving bowl.

In a jar, combine juice, sesame oil, vegetable oil, vinegar, sugar, red pepper flakes and salt. Secure lid; shake vigorously until well blended. Pour dressing over spinach and onion; toss gently yet thoroughly to coat completely. Add strawberries; toss gently. Serve topped with almonds and goat cheese, if desired.

Variation: For a refreshing addition, add 1 to 2 teaspoons grated fresh ginger to the salad dressing.

whoopie pies

MAKES 10 TO 15 SERVINGS

½	cup shortening
2	cups all-purpose flour
⅔	cup unsweetened cocoa powder
1	teaspoon baking soda
½	teaspoon salt
1	teaspoon lemon juice
1¼	cups milk
1	cup sugar
1½	teaspoons vanilla
1	egg
¼	cup shelled pistachio nuts, finely ground in food processor or by hand
1	pint heavy whipping cream
1	can (16 ounces) dark chocolate frosting
	Additional shelled and chopped pistachio nuts (optional)

In large mixing bowl, beat shortening on high speed with Oster® Hand Mixer. In a separate bowl, combine flour, cocoa, baking soda and salt. In glass measuring cup, whisk lemon juice into milk 30 seconds or until combined.

Add half of flour mixture, half of milk mixture and all sugar, vanilla and egg to shortening. Beat until well mixed. Add remaining flour mixture, ¼ cup pistachio nuts and remaining milk mixture and beat until blended.

Drop batter by ½ cupfuls 2 inches apart onto ungreased cookie sheet. Bake at 350°F 15 to 20 minutes or until edges are firm. Cool.

Whip cream with Oster® Hand Mixer. Spoon or pipe onto flat side of 1 cookie. Place another cookie (rounded side up) on top of cream. Repeat with remaining cookies and cream. Heat frosting in microwave on HIGH until just melted. Immediately pour over prepared pies. Garnish with pistachio nuts.

Oster

Entertaining Tip

Cookies and whipped cream may be prepared several hours in advance, but do not assemble until just before serving or cookies will become soggy.

tri-color cauliflower

MAKES 4 SERVINGS

3 heads cauliflower (each a different color, if available)	
¼ cup heavy cream	
3 tablespoons prepared garlic butter*	
2 teaspoons arrowroot powder	

*Or make your own garlic butter by stirring 1 or 2 finely minced garlic cloves into 3 tablespoons room temperature butter. Refrigerate in airtight container several hours or overnight to allow flavor to develop to its fullest, or use immediately.

Cook cauliflower 15 minutes in Oster® Food Steamer. Remove from steamer. Transfer to serving platter and keep warm.

Place cream, garlic butter and arrowroot in rice bowl that comes with steamer; stir. Cover and steam 7 minutes. Remove bowl from steamer and stir sauce until smooth.

Oster

Entertaining Tip

In addition to the well-known white variety, cauliflower is available in purple and green varieties. Check with the manager of the produce department of your favorite grocery store.

chocolate strawberry cream cake

MAKES 14 SERVINGS

2 cups all-purpose flour
2 cups plus 3 tablespoons sugar, divided
½ cup unsweetened cocoa powder
2 teaspoons baking soda
½ teaspoon salt
1 cup warm water
½ cup vegetable oil
½ cup (1 stick) butter, melted
2 eggs, at room temperature
½ cup buttermilk
3 teaspoons vanilla, divided
1 cup (6 ounces) semisweet chocolate chips
1½ cups plus 3 tablespoons cold whipping cream, divided
½ cup strawberry jam
3 tablespoons cold sour cream
Fresh strawberries (optional)

Preheat oven to 350°F. Coat 2 (9-inch) round baking pans with nonstick cooking spray. Line with parchment paper; spray with cooking spray.

Beat flour, 2 cups sugar, cocoa, baking soda and salt in large bowl with Oster® Hand Mixer on low speed about 30 seconds. Beat water, oil, melted butter, eggs, buttermilk and 2 teaspoons vanilla in separate bowl until well blended. Pour butter mixture into dry ingredients and beat on low speed 2 minutes. Pour into prepared pans.

Bake 35 to 40 minutes or until toothpick inserted into centers comes out clean. Cool in pans on wire racks 15 minutes. Remove pans and cool completely on wire racks. Peel off paper before assembling cake.

Heat chocolate chips and 3 tablespoons cream in microwave on HIGH 40 seconds. Whisk mixture smooth. Set aside to cool slightly

Place 1 cake layer on serving plate. Spread with ¼ cup jam. Spread chocolate over jam. Top with second cake layer; spread with remaining jam. Cover loosely with plastic wrap and refrigerate 2 hours or up to 2 days.

Beat remaining 1½ cups cream, remaining 3 tablespoons sugar, remaining 1 teaspoon vanilla and sour cream in large bowl just until stiff peaks form. (Do not overbeat.) Spread on top and sides of cake. Refrigerate until ready to serve, up to 8 hours. Garnish with strawberries.

real pan-fried chicken

MAKES 6 SERVINGS

1	whole chicken, cut into 8 pieces
2	quarts water
4½	tablespoons sea salt, divided
1	quart buttermilk (preferably from whole milk)
2	cups all-purpose flour
½	cup cornstarch
¼	cup potato flour
½	teaspoon black pepper
	Special Chicken-Frying Fat (recipe follows)

Combine chicken, water and 3 tablespoons salt in bowl and refrigerate 8 hours or overnight.

Remove chicken from water brine and cover with buttermilk. Combine with 1 tablespoon salt. Let chicken rest in buttermilk at least 2 hours or overnight.

Remove chicken from buttermilk mixture. With hands, squeeze or wipe off any remaining buttermilk. This will leave a light coating.

Mix all-purpose flour, cornstarch, potato flour, remaining ½ tablespoon salt and pepper. Very lightly dredge chicken in mixture. Take care to cover thoroughly, but shake well to remove excess.

Heat Special Chicken-Frying Fat to 350°F in Oster® Electric Skillet. Fry chicken pieces, skin side down first, 5 to 6 minutes on each side or until golden and cooked through, taking care not to crowd pieces in pan. Drain on paper towels and serve.

special chicken-frying fat

1½	pounds fresh, high-quality lard
1	cup (2 sticks) unsalted butter
2	thick slices cured pork shoulder or country ham

Combine lard, butter and ham slices in large saucepan over medium heat. Cook until fat is melted. Skim off and discard foam. Pour clear butter into bowl to separate from milk solids on bottom. Discard milk solids. Cool clarified fat; strain solids and use for frying chicken. Store in airtight container in refrigerator; do not reuse.

skillet tuscan pork
with fresh tomatoes

MAKES 4 SERVINGS

2	tablespoons butter
2	tablespoons olive oil
¼	cup all-purpose flour
1	teaspoon salt
¾	teaspoon seasoned pepper
4	(1-inch-thick) center-cut boneless pork loin chops, butterflied
½	medium onion, chopped
½	red bell pepper, seeded and roughly chopped
3 to 4	garlic cloves, minced
2	medium yellow tomatoes, chopped
3	red tomatoes, chopped
⅓	cup white wine
2	tablespoons chopped fresh rosemary
2	(3-inch) strips orange peel
12	small pitted green olives or small pitted black olives (or a combination)
4	cups cooked pasta
3	tablespoons chopped fresh Italian parsley (optional)
2	green onions, chopped (optional)

Heat butter and oil in Oster® Electric Skillet over high heat.

Combine flour, salt and pepper in shallow dish. Dredge pork chops in flour mixture. Add to Oster® Electric Skillet and cook 3 to 4 minutes or until golden. Flip pork chops and add onion and red bell pepper. Cook 3 to 4 minutes or until pork chops are golden on second side.

Add garlic and sauté about 10 seconds. Add tomatoes and wine, stirring to scrape up browned bits from bottom of pan.

Add rosemary, orange peel and olives. Bring to a simmer and cook 1 minute. Season to taste with salt and pepper.

Add pasta and stir until coated with sauce and heated through. Garnish as desired with Italian parsley or green onions.

Variation: For a spicy sauce, stir in 1 teaspoon red pepper flakes.

Family Celebrations

roasted vegetable salad
with capers and walnuts

MAKES 6 TO 8 SERVINGS

SALAD

1	pound small Brussels sprouts
1	pound very small Yukon Gold potatoes
¼	teaspoon salt
¼	teaspoon black pepper
¼	teaspoon dried rosemary
3	tablespoons olive oil
1	large red bell pepper, cut into bite-size chunks
¼	cup walnuts, coarsely chopped
2	tablespoons capers

DRESSING

2	tablespoons extra-virgin olive oil
1½	tablespoons white wine vinegar
	Salt and black pepper

Preheat oven to 400°F. For salad, wash, trim and pat dry Brussels sprouts. Slash bottoms. Scrub and pat dry potatoes; cut into halves.

Place Brussels sprouts and potatoes in shallow roasting pan; sprinkle with salt, pepper and rosemary. Drizzle with olive oil; toss to coat. Roast 20 minutes. Stir in bell pepper; roast 15 minutes or until vegetables are tender. Transfer to large serving bowl; stir in walnuts and capers.

For dressing, whisk oil and vinegar in small bowl until well blended; add salt and pepper to taste. Pour over salad; toss to coat. Serve at room temperature.

Oster

Entertaining Tip

To bring Roasted Vegetable Salad as a potluck dish, prepare in advance. Cover and refrigerate up to 1 day. Serve at room temperature.

little ribs in paprika sauce

MAKES 6 TO 8 SERVINGS

1 rack (about 1½ pounds) baby back pork ribs, split

1 can (about 14 ounces) chicken broth

1 cup dry white wine or beer

1 tablespoon olive oil

2 teaspoons dried oregano

2 teaspoons smoked paprika or paprika

4 cloves garlic, minced

½ teaspoon salt

¼ teaspoon black pepper

Cut ribs into individual pieces. Place ribs, broth, wine, oil, oregano, paprika, garlic, salt and pepper in large saucepan. Bring to a boil over medium-high heat. Reduce heat. Simmer, covered, 1 hour or until meat is tender and begins to separate from bones.

Remove ribs to serving plate; keep warm. Skim and discard fat from cooking liquid. Bring to a boil over medium heat. Reduce heat. Simmer until sauce is reduced to about 3 tablespoons. Spoon sauce over ribs. Serve immediately.

garlic shrimp casserole

MAKES 6 TO 8 SERVINGS

Butter 8- or 9-inch square baking dish. Sprinkle evenly with bread crumbs. Preheat Oster® Countertop Oven to 325°F.

Peel and devein shrimp; slice lengthwise and set aside. Heat olive oil in medium saucepan over medium heat. Add onion, celery and garlic; cook, stirring, until onions soften. Add rice and stir to evenly coat all ingredients. (Reduce heat, if necessary, to prevent browning ingredients.)

Add broth and bring to a boil. Remove from heat and stir in lemon juice, lemon zest and parsley. Fold in sour cream and shrimp and pour into prepared baking dish. Sprinkle with cheese.

Cover baking dish with foil. Bake in Oster® Countertop Oven 20 minutes. Remove foil and bake 10 minutes more. Serve immediately.

1	tablespoon butter
2	tablespoons bread crumbs
2	pounds shrimp*
1	tablespoon extra-virgin olive oil
1	onion, finely chopped
2	stalks celery, chopped
3	cloves garlic, minced
1½	cups converted rice
3	cups chicken broth
½	tablespoon lemon juice
½	teaspoon grated lemon peel
1	tablespoon chopped fresh Italian parsley
½	cup low-fat sour cream
¼	cup grated Parmesan cheese

*For best results, use U10-size shrimp.

Oster

Entertaining Tip

Shrimp are labelled for sale according to size; "U10 shrimp" means there are about 10 shrimp per pound. You can substitute smaller shrimp if you like without significantly affecting the cook time.

roasted sweet potatoes
with apples & raisins

MAKES 2 TO 3 SERVINGS

1	**large sweet potato, peeled and cut into wedges**
2	**crisp red apples, cored and cut into wedges**
1	**tablespoon oil**
2	**tablespoons honey**
¼	**cup raisins**

Preheat Oster® Countertop Oven to 375°F.

Place potatoes and apples in separate bowls.

In microwave-safe bowl, combine oil and honey. Heat in microwave on HIGH 10 seconds. Pour half of honey-oil sauce over potatoes and half over apples. Toss to coat well.

Place potatoes in roasting pan and bake in Oster® Countertop Oven 25 minutes.

Remove from oven toss with apples and raisins. Bake 30 minutes more or until potatoes are cooked through and glazed.

baked brie
with nut crust

MAKES 8 SERVINGS

Preheat oven to 350°F. Place nuts in Oster® Food Processor fitted with steel blade; pulse to finely chop. **Do not overprocess.** Transfer chopped nuts to shallow dish or pie plate.

Combine egg and cream in another shallow dish; whisk until well blended.

Dip Brie into egg mixture, then into nut mixture, pressing nuts to adhere. Place Brie on baking sheet and spread jam over top. Bake 15 minutes or until Brie is warm and soft.

⅓	cup pecans
⅓	cup almonds
⅓	cup walnuts
1	egg
1	tablespoon heavy cream
1	wheel (8 ounces) Brie cheese
2	tablespoons sugar-free raspberry jam

honey-lemon green & yellow beans

MAKES 8 SERVINGS

1	pound green beans
1	pound yellow wax beans
2	tablespoons butter
2	tablespoons honey
1	tablespoon grated lemon peel
1	teaspoon salt
½	teaspoon black pepper

Bring 2½ quarts salted water to a boil in large saucepan. Add beans; boil 2 minutes. Remove immediately to bowl of ice water. Drain and pat dry.*

Melt butter in large nonstick skillet over medium-high heat. Add beans; cook and stir 2 minutes or until heated through. Add honey; cook 1 minute. Remove from heat and stir in lemon peel, salt and pepper. Serve immediately.

*This can be done several hours ahead. Cover and refrigerate beans until ready to use.

macaroni gratin

MAKES 6 SERVINGS

Preheat Oster® Countertop Oven to 350°F.

Butter 8-inch round baking dish and set aside. Boil potato in large pot of salted water until tender, about 10 minutes. Remove potato from water (or drain in colander) and place in large bowl. Add macaroni to same pot of boiling salted water and cook just until al dente. Drain macaroni. Add to bowl with potato.

Melt 2 tablespoons butter in large skillet over medium-high heat. Add onions and cook, stirring often, until translucent. Add cream and milk and cook 5 minutes. Add thyme and remove from heat. Pour over potatoes and macaroni. Add both cheeses and mix well. Season to taste with salt and pepper. Transfer to prepared baking dish. Bake until heated through and cheeses are melted, about 20 minutes. Serve immediately.

2	cups diced and peeled Yukon Gold or russet potatoes
8	ounces uncooked small elbow macaroni
2	tablespoons butter, plus additional to grease baking dish
2	cups diced Spanish onions
1	cup whipping cream
¾	cup milk
1	tablespoon chopped fresh thyme
1	cup grated Parmesan cheese
1½	cups (6 ounces) shredded Swiss cheese
	Salt and black pepper

Oster

Entertaining Tip

This casserole makes a tasty side for nearly any roasted meat, and it can be prepared up to 1 day in advance. Just reheat in a 325°F oven for about 20 minutes or until warmed through.

chicken meatballs
with chipotle-honey sauce

MAKES 48 MEATBALLS

2 pounds ground chicken
2 eggs, lightly beaten
⅓ cup plain dry bread crumbs
⅓ cup chopped fresh cilantro
2 tablespoons fresh lime juice
4 cloves garlic, minced
1 can (4 ounces) whole chipotle peppers in adobo sauce, divided
1 teaspoon salt
2 tablespoons vegetable oil
Chipotle-Honey Sauce (recipe follows)

Line 2 baking sheets with parchment paper. Combine ground chicken, eggs, bread crumbs, cilantro, lime juice, garlic, 1 tablespoon adobo sauce (reserve peppers for sauce) and salt in medium bowl; mix well. Form meat mixture into 48 meatballs. Place meatballs on prepared baking sheets. Cover with plastic wrap; chill 1 hour.

Preheat oven to 400°F. Prepare Chipotle-Honey sauce. Lightly coat meatballs with oil using pastry brush. Bake 12 minutes. Remove meatballs to baking dish. Add sauce to dish; stir until coated. Bake 10 minutes or until meatballs are hot and glazed with sauce.

chipotle-honey sauce

¾ cup honey
2 to 3 whole chipotle peppers in adobo sauce, drained
⅓ cup chicken broth
⅓ cup tomato paste
1 tablespoon lime juice
2 teaspoons Dijon mustard
½ teaspoon salt

Combine all ingredients in Oster® Food Processor or Blender; process until smooth.

cheesecake cookie bars

MAKES ABOUT 2 DOZEN BARS

2 packages (18 ounces each) refrigerated chocolate chip cookie dough

2 packages (8 ounces each) cream cheese, softened

½ cup sugar

2 eggs

Preheat oven to 350°F. Lightly grease 13×9-inch baking pan. Let both packages of dough stand at room temperature about 15 minutes.

Reserve three fourths of 1 package dough. Press remaining 1¼ packages dough evenly onto bottom of prepared pan.

Combine cream cheese, sugar and eggs in large bowl; beat until well blended and smooth. Spread cream cheese mixture over dough in pan. Break reserved dough into small pieces; sprinkle over cream cheese mixture.

Bake 35 minutes or until center is almost set. Cool completely in pan on wire rack. Store leftovers covered in refrigerator.

chocolate waffle cookies

MAKES ABOUT 8 DOZEN COOKIES

Beat butter and sugar together with Oster® Hand Mixer in large bowl. Add eggs and vanilla and continue beating until light and fluffy. Blend in melted chocolate. Add flour and mix well. Stir in semisweet and white chocolate chips.

Drop dough by tablespoonfuls 1 inch apart onto preheated Oster® Wafflemaker (4 or 5 cookies can usually be made at a single time based on size of waffle iron). Bake about 1 minute or until golden. Lift out cookies carefully and place on wire rack to cool. Dust lightly with powdered sugar and serve.

½	cup (1 stick) butter or margarine, softened
1	cup granulated sugar
2	eggs
1	teaspoon vanilla
2	squares (1 ounce each) unsweetened chocolate, melted
1	cup all-purpose flour
½	cup semisweet chocolate chips
½	cup white chocolate chips
	Powdered sugar

Oster®

Entertaining Tip

Whipping up an exciting dessert at your next family gathering is easy with a wafflemaker. These cookies are just as easy to make as traditional chocolate chip cookies, but they are so much more fun.

Casual Elegance

espresso mousse

MAKES 8 SERVINGS

¼	cup cold water
2	envelopes unflavored gelatin
½	cup fresh espresso, hot
½	cup boiling water
1	cup semisweet chocolate chips
1	tablespoon sugar
½	teaspoon vanilla
1	cup heavy cream
2	egg yolks
1½	cups ice cubes
	Sweetened whipped cream (optional)
	Chocolate shavings or ground nutmeg (optional)

Combine cold water and gelatin in Oster® Blender container and let stand 2 minutes.

Pour hot espresso and boiling water into blender. Cover, loosen feeder cap and process at PULSE until gelatin is dissolved. Turn unit to ON. Remove feeder cap and add chocolate chips, sugar and vanilla. Continue processing until mixture is smooth.

Add cream, egg yolks and ice. Replace cap and continue processing until mixture begins to thicken. Stop blender and immediately pour into 8 serving dishes. Let stand 5 to 10 minutes before serving. Garnish with sweetened whipped cream and chocolate shavings.

Note: Use an Oster® Blender to pack just the right touch of coffee into this luscious dessert. Combine sugar, gelatin, vanilla, espresso, eggs, cream and chocolate and top with fresh whipped cream and a sprinkle of chocolate shavings or ground nutmeg.

seared tilapia
with black olive salsa

MAKES 4 SERVINGS (1 FILLET PLUS ½ CUP SALSA EACH)

2	plum tomatoes, finely chopped
1	can (4 ounces) chopped black olives, drained
¼	cup finely chopped green onion (green and white parts)
3	tablespoons chopped fresh cilantro
1	medium jalapeño,* seeded and finely chopped
1½	tablespoons extra-virgin olive oil, divided
1	tablespoon lime juice
¼	teaspoon salt
4	tilapia fillets (4 ounces each), rinsed and patted dry
½	teaspoon chili powder
¼	teaspoon seasoned salt
1	medium lime, cut into 8 wedges

Combine tomatoes, olives, green onion, cilantro, jalapeño, 1½ teaspoons oil, lime juice and salt in medium bowl; set aside.

Sprinkle both sides of fillets with chili powder and seasoned salt. Heat remaining 1 tablespoon oil in large nonstick skillet over medium-high heat until hot. Add fillets; cook 3 minutes; turn. Cook 3 to 4 minutes more or until opaque in center. Serve with black olive salsa and lime wedges.

Note: Salsa may be made up to 2 days in advance. Store in refrigerator.

*Jalapeño peppers can sting and irritate the skin; wear rubber gloves when handling peppers and do not touch eyes. Wash hands after handling.

fish bites
with romesco sauce

MAKES 4 SERVINGS

1 slice crusty Italian bread
1 plum tomato, quartered
2 cloves garlic, peeled
3 tablespoons whole almonds, blanched and peeled
2 tablespoons chopped pimiento, drained
1 tablespoon red wine vinegar
¼ teaspoon paprika
¼ teaspoon plus ⅛ teaspoon salt, divided
1 egg white
2 tablespoons all-purpose flour
½ teaspoon ground red pepper
⅓ cup ground almonds
4 tilapia fillets (2 pounds)

Preheat oven to 350°F. Lightly grease baking sheet.

Place bread, tomato, garlic and almonds on baking sheet. Bake 12 to 15 minutes or until almonds are lightly browned. Transfer ingredients to food processor; pulse just until ingredients are coarsely chopped. Add pimiento, vinegar, paprika and ⅛ teaspoon salt. Process until almost smooth. Place sauce in small bowl; set aside.

Lightly beat egg white in small bowl. Combine flour, red pepper and remaining ¼ teaspoon salt in shallow bowl. Place ground almonds in second shallow bowl.

Cut each tilapia fillet into four 1½-inch pieces. Coat fish in flour mixture, shaking off excess. Dip into egg white; roll in almonds until evenly coated.

Arrange fish on baking sheet. Bake 18 to 20 minutes or until fish is golden and flakes when tested with fork. Serve immediately with sauce.

Note: Slivered almonds can be substituted for the whole almonds. In step 2, bake them on a separate baking pan 8 minutes or until lightly browned, stirring once.

Casual Elegance

moroccan stir-fry

MAKES 4 (½-CUP) SERVINGS

4	**to 6 cloves garlic, minced**
2	**teaspoons ground ginger**
1	**teaspoon ground cumin**
½	**teaspoon ground cinnamon**
1	**medium onion, chopped**
12	**ounces boneless skinless chicken thighs, cut into 1-inch pieces**
1¼	**pounds butternut squash, peeled and cut into 1-inch pieces**
1	**can (14½ ounces) fat-free reduced-sodium chicken broth**
½	**cup raisins**
1	**medium zucchini, cut in half lengthwise and sliced crosswise**
2	**tablespoons chopped fresh cilantro**
1	**cup water**
⅔	**cup uncooked couscous**

Combine garlic, ginger, cumin and cinnamon in small bowl; set aside.

Spray large nonstick skillet with nonstick cooking spray; heat over high heat. Add onion; cook and stir until crisp-tender and golden. Add chicken; cook, without stirring, 1 minute or until golden. Turn chicken; cook 1 minute more. Add spice mixture; stir 30 seconds or until fragrant. Stir in butternut squash, chicken broth and raisins; bring to a boil. Reduce heat to low; simmer, covered, 15 to 20 minutes or until butternut squash is tender when pierced. Add zucchini. Simmer, uncovered, 5 to 7 minutes or until zucchini is tender. Stir in cilantro.

Meanwhile, place water in small saucepan over high heat; bring to a boil. Stir in couscous; cover and remove from heat. Let stand 5 minutes. Fluff couscous with fork; spoon onto serving platter. Arrange chicken mixture over couscous.

Oster

Entertaining Tip

Decorate your table to match the meal by using vibrant colors and tiered candles. Show your inner creativity with name cards placed in small picture frames.

mini crab and goat cheese empanadas
with mango chutney

MAKES ABOUT 24 SERVINGS

2 cups all-purpose flour
1 teaspoon salt
½ cup (1 stick) plus 2 tablespoons butter, cut into small cubes
⅓ cup cold water
1 tablespoon olive oil
1 Spanish onion, chopped
3 cloves garlic, minced
¼ habañero pepper, seeded and minced
1 pound lump crabmeat, picked over for shell pieces and cartilage
1 cup soft goat cheese
¼ cup fresh Italian parsley, chopped
1 teaspoon fresh thyme, chopped
Mango Chutney (recipe follows)

Combine flour, salt and butter in Oster® Food Processor. Process until becomes coarse meal. Add water and pulse until smooth dough forms. Transfer to small bowl and cover with slightly damp cloth. Allow dough to rest at least 20 minutes.

Heat olive oil in large skillet over medium heat. Add onion, garlic and habañero pepper. Transfer to large bowl. Add crabmeat, goat cheese, parsley and thyme and toss to combine.

Roll dough out to about ⅛-inch thickness on lightly floured surface. Cut out 3-inch circles with round cookie cutter. Place about 2 teaspoons filling into center of each circle. Moisten exposed dough with a finger dipped in water. Fold empanadas in half, pressing firmly to seal, and crimp with fork around edges.

Fry empanadas in Oster® Deep Fryer according to manufacturer's instructions. Alternatively, heat 1½ to 2 inches vegetable oil in deep pot over medium-high heat. Fry empanadas 2 or 3 at a time until golden brown. Remove from pot with slotted spoon and drain on wire rack. Serve warm with Mango Chutney.

mango chutney

Combine all ingredients except cornstarch in Oster® Electric Skillet. Cook 30 minutes. For thicker chutney, stir cornstarch into 2 tablespoons water, then stir into chutney. Cook another 3 to 4 minutes until thickened. Serve with empanadas.

MAKES ABOUT 1½ CUPS

2	mangoes, peeled, seeded and chopped
1	tablespoon minced fresh ginger
¼	Spanish onion, chopped
1	tablespoon rice wine vinegar
2	tablespoons sugar
1	tablespoon cornstarch (optional)

Oster

Entertaining Tip

Oster® deep fryers can help minimize the hassle and the mess associated with frying foods at home. Many models even incorporate integrated filters to help reduce splattering and odors.

crab-stuffed portobello mushrooms

MAKES 8 SERVINGS

- **8 ounces canned crabmeat, picked over for shell pieces and cartilage**
- **¼ cup thinly sliced green onion**
- **3 tablespoons minced fresh dill**
- **½ small red bell pepper, seeded and finely chopped**
- **½ teaspoon kosher salt**
- **Black pepper to taste**
- **Juice of ½ lemon**
- **½ teaspoon seafood seasoning**
- **¼ cup mayonnaise**
- **¼ cup heavy cream**
- **1 cup dry seasoned cornbread stuffing mix**
- **8 portobello mushroom caps**
- **Olive oil**
- **8 single-serving 1-inch cheese rounds**
- **½ cup grated Parmesan cheese**
- **Lemon wedges (optional)**

Preheat Oster® Countertop Oven to 400°F.

Combine crabmeat, green onion, dill, red bell pepper, salt, black pepper, lemon juice, seafood seasoning, mayonnaise, heavy cream and stuffing mix in large bowl. Fold gently to combine; do not overmix.

Brush portobello mushrooms clean. Scrape dark gills from undersides of mushroom caps with spoon. Place 4 mushroom caps bottom side up on baking tray. Drizzle or brush with olive oil.

Place 1 whole cheese round in center of each mushroom cap. Mound one eighth of crabmeat mixture on top of each mushroom cap, smoothing to cover cheese. Sprinkle with about 1 ½ teaspoons Parmesan cheese. Drizzle with additional olive oil. Bake 25 to 30 minutes or until golden on top and mushrooms are cooked through. Remove from oven and serve immediately; repeat with remaining ingredients to make 4 more stuffed mushroom caps.

roasted sweet potato & hoisin lettuce wraps

MAKES 4 SERVINGS

*Matchstick carrots are sometimes called shredded carrots and may be sold with other prepared vegetables in the supermarket produce section.

Preheat oven to 425°F. Line baking sheet with aluminum foil. Place potatoes and onion on baking sheet. Drizzle with oil. Toss gently to coat vegetables evenly. Bake 10 minutes. Stir and bake 10 minutes longer or until onions begin to brown on edges and potatoes are tender.

To serve, top each lettuce leaf with cabbage, sweet potato mixture and carrots. Drizzle with 1 tablespoon Hoisin Dressing and sprinkle with peanuts. Fold bottom over filling, then fold two sides up to form bundles.

1 to 2	sweet potatoes (about ¾ pound), peeled and cut into ½-inch cubes
1	large onion, cut into 8 wedges
1	tablespoon vegetable oil
12	large Boston Bibb lettuce leaves, rinsed and patted dry
2	cups shredded cabbage or packaged coleslaw
½	cup matchstick carrots*
	Hoisin Dressing (recipe follows)
½	cup peanuts, toasted

hoisin dressing

Combine all ingredients in small bowl. Whisk until well blended; set aside until needed.

MAKES ABOUT ¾ CUP DRESSING

¼	cup creamy peanut butter
3	tablespoons hoisin sauce
1	tablespoon vegetable oil
1	tablespoon ketchup
¼	cup water
2	tablespoons lime juice
3	cloves garlic, minced
2	teaspoons grated fresh ginger
⅛	teaspoon red pepper flakes

beer-braised osso bucco

MAKES 4 SERVINGS

½ **cup all-purpose flour**

1 **teaspoon salt**

½ **teaspoon black pepper**

4 **veal shanks, cut into 1-inch rounds (about 3 pounds)**

3 **tablespoons canola oil**

3 **carrots, chopped**

3 **celery stalks, chopped**

1 **large onion, sliced**

2 **cloves garlic, minced**

2 **tablespoons tomato paste**

1 **bottle (12 ounces) beer**

2 **cups beef broth**

1 **bay leaf**

Grated peel of 1 lemon

Salt and black pepper

Mashed potatoes or cooked polenta

Chopped fresh parsley

Preheat oven to 325°F. In medium bowl, combine flour, salt and pepper. Add veal shanks and turn to coat with flour mixture.

In large ovenproof saucepan or Dutch oven, heat canola oil over medium-high heat until hot. Brown veal shanks on all sides, 2 at a time, about 4 to 6 minutes per side. Remove and set aside. Reduce heat to medium. Add carrots, celery and onion; cook until softened, stirring frequently, about 5 minutes. Add garlic; cook 1 minute more. Stir in tomato paste. Add beer, scraping browned bits from bottom of pan with wooden spoon. Return shanks to pan.

Add broth, bay leaf, zest, salt and pepper to saucepan. Bring to a boil over high heat; remove and cover tightly. Bake in oven 2½ to 3 hours or until fork tender. Remove shanks from saucepan and place in soup bowls. Place scoop of mashed potatoes next to shanks. Strain sauce and boil until reduced to about 2 cups. Pour ½ cup sauce over meat and potatoes. Sprinkle with chopped parsley.

hot & sweet deviled eggs

MAKES 12 SERVINGS

6	**hard-cooked eggs, peeled and cut lengthwise into halves**
4 to 5 tablespoons	**mayonnaise**
¼ teaspoon curry powder	
¼ teaspoon black pepper	
⅛ teaspoon salt	
Dash paprika	
¼	**cup dried sweet cherries or cranberries, finely chopped**
1	**teaspoon minced fresh chives, plus additional for garnish**

Scoop egg yolks into bowl; reserve whites. Mash yolks with fork. Add mayonnaise and beat with fork until creamy. Stir in curry powder, pepper, salt and paprika; mix well. Stir in cherries and minced chives.

Spoon or pipe yolk mixture into egg whites. Garnish with additional fresh chives.

pork tenderloin
with molasses, bacon and porcini vinaigrette

MAKES 4 SERVINGS

6	tablespoons porcini mushroom-infused olive oil, divided
1	pork tenderloin (2 pounds)
	Salt and black pepper
½	pound bacon, diced
1	tablespoon finely chopped garlic
1	teaspoon finely chopped fresh rosemary *or* ½ teaspoon dried rosemary
⅓	cup balsamic vinegar
2	tablespoons dark molasses
1	bunch baby spinach, washed
1	tablespoon finely chopped fresh Italian parsley

Preheat oven to 400°F.

Heat 3 tablespoons porcini oil in Oster® Electric Skillet on medium-high heat. Season pork with salt and pepper and cook in skillet 3 to 5 minutes until browned on all sides. Transfer to roasting pan.

Pour cooking juices from skillet over meat and roast in oven about 15 minutes or until internal temperature reaches 165°F. Remove pork from oven, transfer to platter and keep warm.

Heat skillet to medium heat and add bacon. Cook until crisp. Remove bacon from pan and cool on paper towels. Drain off and discard all but 2 tablespoons bacon drippings from skillet. Add garlic and sauté over medium-high heat until light brown. Add rosemary and stir. Turn off skillet, add vinegar and scrape all browned bits from bottom of skillet. Add molasses and stir well. Add spinach and sauté until wilted. Adjust seasoning. To finish sauce, return skillet to heat and stir in juices that have accumulated around pork. Add cooked bacon, parsley and remaining 3 tablespoons porcini oil. Keep warm until serving. To serve, slice meat ¼ inch thick and arrange on heated plates. Spoon sauce over meat.

calamari salad

MAKES 6 SERVINGS

¼ cup plus **1 tablespoon** extra-virgin olive oil, divided

1½ **pounds cleaned fresh squid, tentacles removed**

Juice of 1 lemon

1 **can (about 15 ounces) cannellini beans, rinsed and drained**

1 **cup thinly sliced celery**

1 **cup thinly sliced red bell pepper**

½ **cup thinly sliced white onion**

3 **tablespoons red wine vinegar**

2 **tablespoons chopped fresh Italian parsley**

1 **tablespoon chopped fresh basil**

1 **tablespoon chopped fresh oregano**

2 **cloves garlic, finely chopped**

1 **teaspoon salt**

½ **teaspoon red pepper flakes**

Heat 1 tablespoon oil in large nonstick skillet over medium-high heat. Cook squid until opaque, about 2 minutes per side. Let cool slightly; cut into rings. Place in large bowl; drizzle with lemon juice. Add beans, celery, bell pepper and onion.

Whisk together vinegar, parsley, basil, oregano, garlic, salt and red pepper flakes in small bowl. Slowly whisk in remaining ¼ cup oil until blended. Pour dressing over squid mixture and toss gently. Refrigerate at least 1 hour. Serve chilled or at room temperature.

one-bite burgers

MAKES 36 MINI BURGERS

1 package (11 ounces) refrigerated breadstick dough (12 breadsticks)

1 pound 80% to 85% lean ground beef

2 teaspoons hamburger seasoning mix

12 slices Cheddar or American cheese, quartered (optional)

36 dill pickle slices

Ketchup and/or mustard

Preheat oven to 375°F. Separate dough into 12 breadsticks; cut each breadstick into 3 equal pieces. Tuck ends of each piece under to meet at center, forming buns about 1 ½ inches in diameter and ½ inch high.

Place buns seam side down on ungreased baking sheet. Bake 11 to 14 minutes or until golden brown. Remove to wire racks.

Meanwhile, gently mix ground beef and seasoning mix in large bowl. Shape beef mixture into 36 patties.

Heat large skillet over medium heat. Place half of patties in skillet; cook 4 minutes on one side or until browned. Turn and cook 3 minutes or until burgers are cooked through; top with cheese, if desired. Repeat with remaining patties.

To assemble, split buns in half crosswise. Top bottom halves with burgers, pickle slices, small dollops of ketchup and/or mustard and tops of buns.

fool-proof pavlova
with fresh fruit

MAKES 6 TO 8 SERVINGS

Cut parchment paper to fit baking tray of Oster® Countertop Oven. Draw 8- or 9-inch circle on uncoated side of paper. Turn paper over and wet slightly. Crumple parchment paper into ball; uncrumple and smooth onto baking tray.

Preheat oven to 200°F. Follow manufacturer's instructions to prepare about 3 cups meringue from meringue powder. Spoon into loose mound on prepared parchment paper, using circle as guide. Shape shallow well in center of mound. Bake 1 hour, taking care not to brown meringue. After 1 hour, turn oven off but leave meringue in oven until completely cool, several hours or overnight.

Meanwhile, lightly beat egg whites just until loose but not foamy. Dip fruits in egg whites, then roll in sugar. Place on waxed paper or parchment paper lined baking sheets to dry.

To serve, beat whipping cream to stiff peaks. Spoon whipped cream into meringue shell and top with fruit. Serve immediately.

1	container meringue powder*
2	egg whites
2	cups small, whole fruits (such as berries, grapes, figs and star fruit)
1	cup superfine sugar
1	pint whipping cream

*Meringue powder is available in the baking products aisle of most large supermarkets and from many sources online.

Oster

Entertaining Tip

To whip cream in advance, pour cream into bowl and sprinkle with ½ teaspoon unflavored gelatin. Refrigerate for 10 to 15 minutes to allow gelatin to bloom. Remove from refrigerator and beat to stiff peaks. Cover and refrigerate until needed.

chicken with rice & asparagus pilaf

MAKES 4 SERVINGS

4 **boneless skinless chicken breasts**
3 **teaspoons poultry seasoning, divided**
2 **tablespoons olive oil**
1 **medium onion, chopped**
1 **cup uncooked rice**
1 **clove garlic, minced**
2 **cups chicken broth**
¾ **teaspoon salt**
1 **pound asparagus, trimmed and cut into 2-inch pieces (about 3 cups)**

Sprinkle each chicken breast with ¼ teaspoon poultry seasoning. Heat oil in large skillet over medium-high heat. Brown chicken about 2 minutes on each side. Remove from skillet.

Add onion to skillet; cook and stir 3 minutes. Add rice and garlic; cook and stir 1 to 2 minutes. Add broth, remaining 2 teaspoons poultry seasoning and salt. Bring to a boil over high heat. Reduce heat to low; cook, covered, 5 minutes.

Stir in asparagus and chicken. Cook, covered, 10 to 12 minutes or until rice is tender and chicken is cooked through (165°F).

Oster

Entertaining Tip

Try this recipe in your Oster® Electric Skillet. As an added benefit, the Electric Skillet can be set to warm to keep this dish at the optimal serving temperature.

twice-baked potatoes
with sun-dried tomatoes

MAKES 8 SERVINGS

4 large baking potatoes
Vegetable oil
1 container (16 ounces) sour cream
2 cups (8 ounces) shredded Cheddar cheese, divided
⅓ cup sun-dried tomatoes packed in oil, drained and chopped
¼ cup finely chopped green onions, divided
2 tablespoons butter, softened
1 teaspoon salt
½ teaspoon pepper

Preheat oven to 350°F. Scrub potatoes and pat dry with paper towels. Rub potatoes with vegetable oil; bake 1 hour. Cool 30 minutes.

Cut each potato in half. Scrape potato pulp into large bowl, leaving ½-inch-thick shells. Add sour cream, 1½ cups cheese, sun-dried tomatoes, 3 tablespoons green onions, butter, salt and pepper; mix gently. Fill potato shells with mixture.

Bake 15 to 20 minutes or until heated through. Top with remaining ½ cup cheese; bake 5 minutes or until cheese is melted. Sprinkle with remaining 1 tablespoon green onions.

warm crab & fingerling potato salad
with horseradish crème fraîche and baby red oak lettuce

MAKES 4 SERVINGS

Rinse potatoes and sort by size. Place potatoes in large saucepan with largest on bottom and smaller potatoes on top. Cover potatoes with cold water. Bring to a boil over medium-high heat and simmer about 35 minutes or until potatoes are cooked through. Drain potatoes and cool slightly. Cut into ¼-inch slices and set aside.

Season crème fraîche with salt, white pepper, ground red pepper and lemon juice to taste. Add horseradish, flat chives, shallots and parsley. Mix thoroughly, then gently fold in crabmeat.

Toss warm potatoes gently but thoroughly with crabmeat mixture; add peppercress. Place some mixture in center of each of 4 dinner plates. Lay baby lettuce leaves around dishes. Garnish with onion sprouts and garlic blossoms.

Note: Peppercress is a spicy type of watercress; if it is unavailable watercress may be substituted.

8	fingerling potatoes, assorted sizes
8	Red Bliss potatoes, assorted sizes
3	ounces crème fraîche
	Kosher salt
	White pepper
	Ground red pepper
	Lemon juice
½	teaspoon prepared horseradish
½	teaspoon finely chopped flat chives
3	tablespoons finely diced shallots
½	teaspoon finely chopped fresh Italian parsley
1	pound Maryland lump crabmeat, picked over for shell pieces and cartilage
½	teaspoon peppercress
12	baby red oak lettuce leaves
½	teaspoon onion sprouts (optional)
4	garlic blossoms (optional)

Holiday Cool

seared beef tenderloin
with horseradish-rosemary cream

MAKES 4 SERVINGS

SEARED BEEF TENDERLOIN

1	**beef tenderloin (1 pound)**
1	**clove garlic, halved**
1	**teaspoon chili powder**
¼	**teaspoon salt**
¼	**teaspoon black pepper**

HORSERADISH-ROSEMARY CREAM

⅓	**cup fat-free sour cream**
3	**tablespoons fat-free (skim) milk**
2	**teaspoons reduced-fat mayonnaise**
1	**teaspoon prepared horseradish**
¼	**teaspoon dried rosemary**
¼	**teaspoon salt**
⅛	**teaspoon black pepper**

Preheat oven to 425°F.

Rub tenderloin with garlic halves.

Combine chili powder, salt and pepper in small bowl. Sprinkle mixture evenly over tenderloin.

Heat an ovenproof, medium nonstick skillet over medium-high heat. Coat skillet with nonstick cooking spray. Add tenderloin and cook 2 minutes on each side.

Place skillet and tenderloin in oven. Cook 30 minutes or until tenderloin's internal temperature reaches 140°F. Remove from oven and let rest 15 minutes.

Meanwhile, combine Horseradish-Rosemary Cream ingredients in small bowl.

Slice tenderloin into 12 pieces. Top with Horseradish-Rosemary Cream.

curried pumpkin-apple soup

MAKES 5 TO 6 SERVINGS

2 cups vegetable broth, divided

1 vial (5 grams or about ⅕ ounce) saffron

¼ teaspoon salt

2 cups cubed, peeled, cooked fresh pumpkin (about 1 pound)

1 cored, peeled apple, cut into eighths

½ cored, cubed pear, cut into quarters

2 carrots, peeled and quartered lengthwise

3 green onions, quartered (green parts only)

2 tablespoons butter

1 sprig fresh rosemary, plus additional for garnish (optional)

½ to 1 teaspoon curry powder, or to taste

¼ teaspoon ground nutmeg, plus additional for garnish (optional)

3 tablespoons all-purpose flour

1 cup heavy cream

Roasted pumpkin seeds (optional)

Heat 1 cup broth in microwave until hot. Stir in saffron and set aside.

Add remaining 1 cup broth, salt and cooked pumpkin to Oster® Blender jar and cover with lid. Press ON, then press FOOD CHOP and process to end of cycle.

Remove lid and add apple, pear, carrots and green onion. Replace lid, press FOOD CHOP and process to desired consistency.

Melt butter in 2-quart saucepan over medium heat. Add 1 sprig rosemary, curry powder and ¼ teaspoon nutmeg; cook 30 seconds. Stir in flour; cook 30 seconds. Stir blended pumpkin mixture into pan and stir well to combine. Cover and reduce heat. Simmer 15 to 20 minutes or until carrots are tender, stirring occasionally. Remove from heat and stir in cream. Garnish with seeds, additional rosemary sprig and additional nutmeg.

Note: To serve in a pumpkin shell, cut off the top of a small (2- to 3-pound) pumpkin. Scrape inside of the pumpkin clean, saving seeds to roast later, if desired. Cover top of pumpkin with foil and bake 30 minutes at 350°F or just until tender. Do not overbake or pumpkin will leak.

mini smoked salmon latkes

MAKES ABOUT 24 APPETIZERS

2 cups frozen shredded hash brown potatoes, thawed and drained

2 tablespoons finely chopped shallots

1 egg, lightly beaten

1 tablespoon all-purpose flour

1 tablespoon whipping cream

½ teaspoon salt

¼ teaspoon black pepper

1 tablespoon butter, divided

1 tablespoon vegetable oil, divided

1 package (4 ounces) smoked salmon, cut into 24 pieces

Sour cream

Black whitefish caviar (optional)

Place potatoes on large cutting board and chop into smaller pieces. Combine potatoes, shallots, egg, flour, cream, salt and pepper in large bowl; mix well.

Heat half of butter and oil in Oster® Electric Skillet on medium-high heat. Spoon tablespoonfuls of potato mixture into skillet; flatten with spatula to make small pancakes. Cook about 3 minutes on each side. Repeat with remaining butter, oil and potato mixture.

Top each pancake with small piece of smoked salmon, tiny dollop of sour cream and pinch of caviar, if desired. Serve immediately.

Entertaining Tip

Pair this appetizer with a chilled vodka martini. Use wine charms and have your guests take home the glass and charm as a remembrance of the evening.

brussels sprouts
with walnuts

MAKES 4 SERVINGS

1 pound Brussels sprouts, trimmed

1 cup apple juice

2 cups water

1 cup diced peeled butternut squash (1-inch cubes)

½ cup fat-free vinaigrette salad dressing

1 cup arugula, mixed baby lettuce or baby spinach leaves

½ cup chopped walnuts, toasted

Combine sprouts, apple juice and water in medium saucepan. Simmer over medium heat until sprouts are tender, about 15 minutes. Rinse in cool water and drain well.

Preheat oven to 400°F. Lightly coat baking sheet with nonstick cooking spray. Roast squash on baking sheet 20 minutes or until tender. Remove from oven and cool 5 minutes.

When cool enough to handle, slice sprouts lengthwise into thin slices. Mix with warm squash and toss with fat-free dressing.

Divide arugula among 4 serving plates. Spoon vegetables over greens and sprinkle with walnuts.

manchego cheese croquettes

MAKES 6 SERVINGS

¼ cup (½ stick) butter or margarine

1 tablespoon minced shallots or onion

½ cup all-purpose flour

¾ cup milk

½ cup grated manchego cheese or Parmesan cheese, divided

¼ teaspoon salt

¼ teaspoon smoked paprika or paprika

⅛ teaspoon ground nutmeg

1 egg

½ cup bread crumbs

Vegetable oil

Melt butter in medium skillet over medium heat. Add shallots; cook and stir 2 minutes. Stir in flour; cook and stir 2 minutes. Gradually whisk in milk; cook until mixture comes to a boil. Remove from heat. Stir in ¼ cup cheese, salt, paprika and nutmeg.

Spoon mixture into small bowl; cover and refrigerate several hours or up to 24 hours.

With lightly floured hands, shape teaspoonfuls of dough into 1-inch balls.

Beat egg in shallow bowl. Combine bread crumbs and remaining ¼ cup cheese in second shallow bowl. Dip each ball first into egg, then roll in bread crumb mixture.

Heat vegetable oil in Oster® Deep Fryer to 375°F. Cook croquettes 4 to 6 at a time in batches until brown on all sides. Serve warm with toothpicks.

Note: Cooked croquettes may be kept warm in a 200°F oven up to 30 minutes before serving.

Oster

Entertaining Tip

Be sure to allow the oil a few minutes to reheat between batches.

chocolate almond cream cheese tart

MAKES 16 SERVINGS

¼ cup (½ stick) butter

1½ cups chocolate-covered mint cookie crumbs

½ cup plus 2 tablespoons sugar, divided

¾ cup slivered almonds, toasted*

4 ounces dark chocolate, broken into ½-inch pieces

1 package (8 ounces) cream cheese

2 egg yolks

¼ cup heavy cream

1 tablespoon coffee-flavored liqueur

Whipped cream (optional)

Fresh raspberries (optional)

*To toast almonds, spread in single layer on baking sheet. Bake in preheated 350°F oven 8 to 10 minutes or until golden brown, stirring frequently.

Preheat oven to 350°F.

Place butter, cookie crumbs and 1 tablespoon sugar in Oster® Blender jar and cover jar with lid. Push ON, then push MEDIUM/BLEND and process until well combined. Transfer to 9-inch tart pan or pie plate. Pat evenly into bottom and up sides of pan.

Clean Oster® Blender jar. Add almonds to Oster® Blender jar and cover jar with lid. Push FOOD CHOP and process to end of cycle. Remove almonds from jar and set aside.

Add chocolate, cheese, ½ cup sugar, egg yolks, cream and liqueur to Oster® Blender jar and cover jar with lid. Push FOOD CHOP and process to end of cycle. Push MAX PULSE 3 or 4 times until well blended. Pour mixture into prepared crust. Press almonds onto top and sprinkle with remaining 1 tablespoon sugar. Bake 20 to 25 minutes or until set. Garnish with whipped cream and raspberries.

fruited corn pudding

MAKES 8 TO 10 SERVINGS

5	**cups frozen corn, thawed and divided**
5	**eggs**
½	**cup milk**
1½	**cups whipping cream**
⅓	**cup unsalted butter, melted and cooled**
1	**teaspoon vanilla**
½	**teaspoon salt**
¼	**teaspoon ground nutmeg**
3	**tablespoons finely chopped dried apricots**
3	**tablespoons dried cranberries or raisins**
3	**tablespoons finely chopped dates**
2	**tablespoons finely chopped dried pears or other dried fruit**

Preheat oven to 350°F. Grease 13×9-inch baking dish; set aside.

Combine 3½ cups corn, eggs and milk in Oster® Food Processor; cover and process until mixture is almost smooth.

Transfer corn mixture to large bowl. Add cream, butter, vanilla, salt and nutmeg; stir until well blended. Add remaining 1½ cups corn, apricots, cranberries, dates and pears; stir well. Pour mixture into prepared dish.

Bake 50 to 60 minutes or until pudding is set and top begins to brown. Let stand 10 to 15 minutes before serving.

mushroom stuffing

MAKES 6 TO 8 SERVINGS

Preheat Oster® Countertop Oven to 350°F. Grease shallow 1½-quart casserole dish or 11×9-inch baking pan.

Combine mushrooms, onion, garlic, rosemary and thyme in Oster® Food Processor. Pulse mixture until well minced and thoroughly combined.

Combine 1 tablespoon butter and oil in Oster® Electric Skillet on medium heat. Add mushroom mixture and cook, stirring frequently, about 5 minutes. Add wine and celery; cook another 5 minutes. Add turkey broth and heat through. Turn off heat.

Place cubed bread in very large bowl; pour hot mushroom mixture over bread. Stir to combine until all bread is damp. Spread stuffing evenly in prepared dish. Cover with aluminum foil. Bake 30 minutes. Uncover and bake an additional 15 minutes to brown top. Serve hot.

2 cups mixed fresh mushrooms, trimmed of any tough stems and roughly chopped
½ cup chopped yellow onion
2 cloves garlic
1 tablespoon fresh rosemary
1 tablespoon fresh thyme
1 tablespoon butter, plus additional for greasing casserole dish
1 tablespoon olive oil
1 cup dry white wine or Madeira if available
1 stalk celery, chopped
2 cups turkey or chicken broth
1 quart prepared croutons *or* 1½-inch cubes cut from preferred bread for stuffing

mini cherry kugel

MAKES 12 SERVINGS

1 teaspoon salt, divided

4 ounces (1½ cups) uncooked egg noodles, broken into small pieces

4 eggs

1 cup ricotta cheese

½ cup sour cream

½ cup whipping cream

3 tablespoons sugar

½ cup sweetened dried cherries, chopped

Preheat oven to 350°F. Coat 12 mini (1¾-inch) muffin cups with nonstick cooking spray.

Fill large saucepan three-fourths full with water; add ½ teaspoon salt. Bring to a boil over high heat. Cook noodles according to package directions; drain well and set aside.

Beat eggs, ricotta cheese, sour cream, whipping cream, remaining ½ teaspoon salt and sugar in large bowl with Oster® Hand Mixer on medium speed until blended. Stir in noodles and cherries. Spoon into prepared muffin cups, filling three-fourths full. Bake 50 minutes or until puffed and golden. Cool in pan 1 minute; turn out onto serving platter.

mashed sweet potatoes
with cilantro and lime

MAKES 5 SERVINGS

2 pounds sweet potatoes

⅓ cup milk

2 tablespoons butter

1 teaspoon salt

Dash black pepper

2 tablespoons plus 2 teaspoons lime juice

1 tablespoon chopped fresh cilantro

Pierce potatoes all over with fork; microwave on HIGH about 10 minutes or until tender. Let stand until cool enough to handle.

Combine milk and butter in small saucepan over low heat. Stir until butter is melted; remove from heat.

Remove potato from skins and place in medium bowl; discard skins. Add milk mixture, salt and pepper. Mix with Oster® Hand Mixer on low speed until creamy. Stir in lime juice and cilantro.

MINI CHERRY KUGEL

leg of lamb
with mustard and mint sauce

MAKES ABOUT 8 SERVINGS

1	whole leg of lamb (8 pounds)
	Salt and black pepper
¾	cup Dijon mustard
⅓	cup grainy mustard
4	cloves garlic
¼	cup extra-virgin olive oil
	Dash Worcestershire sauce
1	tablespoon balsamic vinegar
1	tablespoon fresh mint
1	red onion, thinly sliced
2	tablespoons all-purpose flour
4	cups beef broth
	Minted Yogurt Sauce (recipe follows)

Preheat oven to 325°F. Generously salt and pepper lamb.

Combine Dijon mustard, grainy mustard, garlic, olive oil, Worcestershire sauce, balsamic vinegar and mint in Oster® Blender. Purée until well combined. Pour mixture over lamb so that lamb is well coated.

Place lamb in roasting pan; layer onion slices over lamb. Roast, uncovered, to desired doneness (about 20 minutes per pound for medium-rare roast). Transfer lamb to serving platter and cover loosely with foil. Reserve drippings in pan.

Place hot roasting pan with drippings on stovetop. Add flour to hot roasting pan and stir well. Add beef broth and continue stirring until well combined. Carefully pour gravy into small saucepan. Cook gravy over medium-high heat
3 to 4 minutes or until desired consistency. Season to taste with salt and pepper.

Slice lamb and serve with gravy and Minted Yogurt Sauce.

minted yogurt sauce

Combine all ingredients in Oster® Food Processor. Process about 1 minute until well combined but not smooth. Serve cool over warm sliced lamb.

MAKES 1½ CUPS

2	cucumbers, peeled and chopped
2	cloves garlic, chopped
2	tablespoons chopped fresh mint
	Pinch ground cumin
1	cup plain yogurt

pumpkin & parmesan twice-baked potatoes

MAKES 4 SERVINGS

Preheat oven to 400°F. Scrub potatoes; pierce in several places with fork or small knife. Place potatoes directly on oven rack; bake 1 hour or until soft.

When cool enough to handle, cut potatoes in half lengthwise. Scoop out most of potato pulp, leaving thin potato shell.

Spoon potato pulp into medium bowl; mash with fork. Add cheese, half-and-half, pumpkin, sage, salt and pepper; mix well.

Place potato shells on baking sheet; spoon pumpkin mixture into shells. Bake 10 minutes or until filling is heated through.

2	baking potatoes (12 ounces each)
1	cup grated Parmesan cheese
6	tablespoons half-and-half
¼	cup canned pumpkin
1½	teaspoons minced fresh sage *or* ¼ teaspoon dried thyme
¼	teaspoon salt
⅛	teaspoon black pepper

shortbread-crusted cheesecake
with raspberry-ginger sauce

MAKES 12 SERVINGS

- **1 package (10 ounces) shortbread cookies**
- **⅓ cup packed light brown sugar**
- **6 tablespoons butter, cut into cubes and softened**
- **4 packages (8 ounces each) cream cheese, cut into cubes and softened**
- **1 cup granulated sugar, divided**
- **⅛ teaspoon salt**
- **5 eggs**
- **2 teaspoons vanilla**
- **1 package (12 ounces) frozen unsweetened raspberries, thawed**
- **1 teaspoon cornstarch**
- **½ teaspoon grated fresh ginger**

Preheat oven to 350°F. Grind cookies in Oster® Food Processor with on/off pulses to break up cookies. Add brown sugar; pulse to combine. Add butter; pulse until mixture begins to stick together.

Press crumb mixture into bottom and ½ inch up side of 9-inch springform pan. Bake 11 minutes or until lightly browned. Place on wire rack to cool slightly.

For filling, place cream cheese, ¾ cup granulated sugar and salt in Oster® Food Processor; process until smooth. Add eggs and vanilla; process until well blended. Pour into crust.

Bake 1 hour or until center is almost set and knife inserted 2 inches from edge comes out clean. Cool on wire rack. Cover loosely with foil and refrigerate overnight.

For sauce, crush raspberries with back of spoon in fine-mesh sieve to release as much juice as possible; discard berries. Pour juice into measuring cup; add enough water to equal 1 cup liquid. Place in small saucepan with remaining ¼ cup granulated sugar and cornstarch; whisk until cornstarch is completely dissolved. Bring to a boil over medium-high heat; boil 1 minute, stirring frequently. Let sauce cool; refrigerate until ready to serve. Stir in ginger just before serving. Spoon sauce over each slice of cheesecake.

peppery green beans

MAKES 8 (½-CUP) SERVINGS

2 tablespoons olive oil, divided

2 teaspoons Worcestershire sauce

½ teaspoon black pepper

½ teaspoon garlic salt

1 pound whole green beans, stemmed, rinsed and patted dry

1 medium onion, cut into ½-inch wedges

1 medium red bell pepper, cut into ½-inch slices

Salt

Preheat oven to 450°F. Line large baking sheet with foil. Combine oil, Worcestershire sauce, black pepper and garlic salt in small bowl; mix well.

Place beans, onion and bell pepper on prepared baking sheet. Pour half of oil mixture over vegetables; toss to coat. Spread vegetables in single layer.

Roast 20 to 25 minutes or until vegetables begin to brown, stirring every 5 minutes. Add remaining oil mixture and salt to taste; toss to coat.

savory bread pudding
with asparagus and dried tomatoes

MAKES 4 TO 5 SERVINGS

Set Oster® Digital Countertop Toaster Oven to Convection Bake function. Set temperature to 350°F. Grease 8-inch square pan.

Heat olive oil in large skillet over medium heat. Add onion, asparagus, leeks and mushrooms; cook until onion just begins to brown. Set aside.

Whisk eggs, cream, milk, salt and pepper in medium bowl. Combine cheeses, tomatoes, parsley and thyme in separate bowl.

Place half of bread pieces in prepared pan. Sprinkle with half of asparagus mixture, then half of cheese mixture. Pour half of egg mixture over layers. Repeat layers.

Let stand 20 minutes, pressing occasionally with spatula to submerge bread pieces.

Bake 30 to 40 minutes until top browns and custard sets. Allow to cool 10 minutes before serving.

2	tablespoons olive oil
½	large **Vidalia onion,** thinly sliced
½	pound **asparagus,** trimmed and cut into 1½-inch lengths (about 2 cups)
⅓	cup **chopped leeks**
1	cup **sliced mushrooms**
3	large **eggs**
1	cup **whipping cream**
1	cup **milk**
1	teaspoon **salt**
½	teaspoon **black pepper**
½	cup (2 ounces) **shredded Gruyère cheese**
½	cup (2 ounces) **crumbled goat cheese**
½	cup (2 ounces) **shredded fontina cheese**
½	cup **dehydrated tomatoes**
¼	cup **chopped fresh parsley**
2	tablespoons **fresh thyme leaves**
4	cups **day old bread,** cut into 1½-inch cubes (hearty bread like oat or multigrain works very well)

beef rib roast
with mushroom-bacon sauce

MAKES 4 TO 6 SERVINGS

4 to 5 large cloves garlic
1 tablespoon chopped fresh thyme
1 tablespoon chopped fresh basil
1 tablespoon kosher salt
1 tablespoon black pepper
3 tablespoons olive oil
1 beef rib roast (2 to 4 ribs), small end, back bone removed and well-trimmed (6 to 8 pounds)
Mushroom-Bacon Sauce (recipe follows)

Place garlic, thyme, basil, salt and pepper in Oster® Food Processor. Process until garlic is finely chopped. Add oil in slow stream, processing until paste forms.

Pat roast dry; place bone side down on rack in shallow roasting pan. Cut several small slits in fat layer across top of roast. Rub garlic paste over entire roast, pressing some paste into slits. Refrigerate, covered, 4 hours or up to 1 day.

Preheat oven to 450°F. Roast beef 20 minutes. *Reduce oven temperature to 350°F.* Roast until meat thermometer inserted into beef registers 140°F for medium-rare, 150°F for medium. Transfer roast to cutting board; cover and let rest 20 minutes before slicing. Reserve pan drippings to make Mushroom-Bacon Sauce.

Oster®

Entertaining Tip

Menu cards placed on top of each napkin immediately engage guests—a nice touch at holiday parties. Menus can be handwritten or designed on a home computer.

mushroom-bacon sauce

Cook bacon in large saucepan over medium heat until golden. Add shallot and cook 2 minutes. Add mushrooms; cook and stir about 8 minutes until bacon is crisp. Set aside.

Combine broth and wine in large saucepan. Bring to a boil; reduce heat and simmer 20 minutes or until mixture is reduced to about 2 cups. (Recipe can be prepared to this point up to 2 days ahead. Cover mushroom mixture and broth in separate containers and refrigerate until needed.)

While roast is resting, place reserved roasting pan over 2 stovetop burners. Add mushroom mixture and broth mixture; cook and stir over medium heat 5 minutes or until sauce is slightly thickened. Whisk in butter; season to taste with salt and pepper. Serve warm.

4	**slices bacon, chopped**
1	**large shallot, diced**
1	**pound fresh mushrooms, sliced**
6	**cups fat-free reduced-sodium chicken broth**
1	**cup dry red wine**
2	**tablespoons butter**
	Salt and pepper

Index

Almond-Coated Scallops.................................. 76

Appetizers

Almond-Coated Scallops............................ 76

Baked Brie with Nut Crust........................ 99

Chicken Meatballs with Chipotle-Honey
Sauce... 102

Chilled Avocado & Gazpacho Soup 20

Chorizo & Artichoke Kabobs with
Mustard Vinaigrette............................... 62

Citrus-Marinated Atlantic Salmon with
Potato Blinis and Garden Greens........ 78

Crab-Stuffed Portobello Mushrooms..... 116

Curried Pumpkin-Apple Soup................. 132

Edamame Hummus.......................................6

Fish Bites with Romesco Sauce.............. 110

Goat Cheese Stuffed Figs........................ 58

Hot & Sweet Deviled Eggs 120

Little Ribs in Paprika Sauce...................... 96

Manchego Cheese Croquettes 138

Mini Cherry Kugel 144

Mini Crab and Goat Cheese Empanadas
with Mango Chutney............................. 114

Mini Smoked Salmon Latkes.................. 134

Moroccan Chicken Turnovers.................. 66

Olive Tapenade... 24

One-Bite Burgers...................................... 124

Shrimp and Scallop Tapas........................ 77

Shrimp, Goat Cheese & Leek Tortilla...... 80

Tangerine Tequila Shrimp...........................8

Wine Biscuits... 60

Baked Brie with Nut Crust 99

Beans

Calamari Salad... 122

Cuban-Style Marinated Skirt Steak.......... 10

Edamame Hummus.......................................6

Honey-Lemon Green & Yellow
Beans 100

Mesquite-Grilled Tiger Prawns with Pesto,
Cannellini Beans, Grilled Radicchio,
Fennel and Confit Tomatoes 74

Peppery Green Beans 150

Beef

Beef Rib Roast with Mushroom-Bacon
Sauce... 152

Beer-Braised Osso Bucco 118

Cuban-Style Marinated Skirt Steak.......... 10

Leg of Lamb with Mustard and Mint
Sauce... 140

One-Bite Burgers 124

Seared Beef Tenderloin with
Horseradish-Rosemary Cream 130

Steak al Forno.. 28

Beef Rib Roast with Mushroom-Bacon
Sauce 152

Beer-Braised Osso Bucco 118

Beverages

Frozen Daiquiri 18

Frozen Margarita... 12

Frozen Mojito 18

Frozen Sunshine 12

Morning Mocha Smoothie 34

Bratwurst Skillet Breakfast 52

Breakfast Rice Pudding 40

Brussels Sprouts with Walnuts 136

Cakes

Chocolate Hazelnut Cupcakes 72

Chocolate Strawberry Cream Cake......... 88

Mini Gingerbread Wheat Cakes.............. 68

Nutty Toffee Ice Cream Cake 22

Shortbread-Crusted Cheesecake with
Raspberry-Ginger Sauce..................... 148

Calamari Salad 122

Cheesecake Cookie Bars.............................. 104

Chicken

Beef Rib Roast with Mushroom-Bacon
Sauce... 152

Chicken Meatballs with Chipotle-Honey
Sauce... 102

Chicken with Mango-Cherry
Chutney... 30

Chicken with Rice & Asparagus Pilaf 126

Garlic Shrimp Casserole 97

Grilled Vegetable Salad with Feta and Olives 21

Lemon Chicken with Moroccan Olives, Pine Nuts, Toasted Garlic & Couscous 70

Little Ribs in Paprika Sauce 96

Moroccan Chicken Turnovers 66

Moroccan Stir-Fry 112

Mushroom Stuffing 143

Real Pan-Fried Chicken 90

Strawberry-Apricot Barbecue Cornish Hens 27

Chicken Meatballs with Chipotle-Honey Sauce 102

Chicken with Mango-Cherry Chutney 30

Chicken with Rice & Asparagus Pilaf 126

Chilled Avocado & Gazpacho Soup 20

Chocolate

Cheesecake Cookie Bars 104

Chocolate Almond Cream Cheese Tart 140

Chocolate Hazelnut Cupcakes 72

Chocolate Strawberry Cream Cake 88

Chocolate Waffle Cookies 105

Espresso Mousse 106

Morning Mocha Smoothie 34

Nutty Toffee Ice Cream Cake 22

Whoopie Pies 84

Chocolate Almond Cream Cheese Tart 140

Chocolate Hazelnut Cupcakes 72

Chocolate Strawberry Cream Cake 88

Chocolate Waffle Cookies 105

Chorizo & Artichoke Kabobs with Mustard Vinaigrette 62

Cinnamon-Nut Bubble Ring 50

Citrus-Marinated Atlantic Salmon with Potato Blinis and Garden Greens 78

Crab-Stuffed Portobello Mushrooms 116

Cranberry Orange Pumpkin Scones with Whipped Maple Butter 36

Cuban-Style Marinated Skirt Steak 10

Curried Pumpkin-Apple Soup 132

Desserts

Breakfast Rice Pudding 40

Cheesecake Cookie Bars 104

Chocolate Almond Cream Cheese Tart 140

Chocolate Hazelnut Cupcakes 72

Chocolate Strawberry Cream Cake 88

Chocolate Waffle Cookies 105

Cinnamon-Nut Bubble Ring 50

Espresso Mousse 106

Fool-Proof Pavlova with Fresh Fruit 125

Grilled Peaches with Nutmeg Pastry Cream 25

Mango-Banana Foster 32

Mascarpone-Mint Ice Cream, Fresh Figs and Vanilla-Lemon Syrup 26

Mini Gingerbread Wheat Cakes 68

Nutty Toffee Ice Cream Cake 22

Shortbread-Crusted Cheesecake with Raspberry-Ginger Sauce 148

Whoopie Pies 84

Dips

Edamame Hummus 6

Olive Tapenade 24

Easy Raspberry-Peach Danish 54

Edamame Hummus 6

Eggs Benedict with Asparagus & Crab 57

Espresso Mousse 106

Fish Bites with Romesco Sauce 110

Fool-Proof Pavlova with Fresh Fruit 125

Fresh Spinach-Strawberry Salad 82

Frozen Daiquiri 18

Frozen Margarita 12

Frozen Mojito 18

Frozen Sunshine 12

Fruited Corn Pudding 142

Garlic Shrimp Casserole 97

Goat Cheese Stuffed Figs 58

Grilled Foods

Chicken with Mango-Cherry
Chutney..................................... 30

Cuban-Style Marinated Skirt Steak.......... 10

Grilled Peaches with Nutmeg Pastry
Cream 25

Grilled Potato Salad 16

Grilled Vegetable Salad with Feta and
Olives 21

Ham & Egg Breakfast Panini 44

Mango-Banana Foster 32

Mesquite-Grilled Tiger Prawns with Pesto,
Cannellini Beans, Grilled Radicchio,
Fennel and Confit Tomatoes 74

Steak al Forno.. 28

Strawberry-Apricot Barbecue Cornish
Hens.. 27

Tangerine Tequila Shrimp.............................8

Grilled Peaches with Nutmeg Pastry
Cream.. 25

Grilled Potato Salad...................................... 16

Grilled Vegetable Salad with Feta
and Olives 21

Ham & Egg Breakfast Panini............................ 44

Ham-Egg-Brie Strudel.................................... 56

Honey Granola with Yogurt 42

Honey-Lemon Green & Yellow Beans........ 100

Honey-Wheat Pancakes 53

Hot & Sweet Deviled Eggs 120

Ice Cream

Mango-Banana Foster 32

Mascarpone-Mint Ice Cream, Fresh Figs
and Vanilla-Lemon Syrup....................... 26

Morning Mocha Smoothie 34

Nutty Toffee Ice Cream Cake 22

Jumbo Lump Crabmeat with Potato
Pancakes, Mango and Baby Greens........ 64

Leg of Lamb with Mustard and Mint
Sauce 146

Lemon Chicken with Moroccan Olives,
Pine Nuts, Toasted Garlic &
Couscous 70

Light 'n' Crisp Waffles................................... 49

Little Ribs in Paprika Sauce 96

Macaroni Gratin.. 101

Main Dishes

Beef Rib Roast with Mushroom-Bacon
Sauce.. 152

Beer-Braised Osso Bucco 118

Bratwurst Skillet Breakfast 52

Breakfast Rice Pudding............................... 40

Chicken Meatballs with Chipotle-Honey
Sauce 102

Chicken with Mango-Cherry
Chutney.................................... 30

Chicken with Rice & Asparagus
Pilaf.. 126

Crab-Stuffed Portobello
Mushrooms 116

Cuban-Style Marinated Skirt
Steak... 10

Eggs Benedict with Asparagus &
Crab.. 57

Garlic Shrimp Casserole............................... 97

Grilled Vegetable Salad with Feta and
Olives... 19

Ham & Egg Breakfast Panini 44

Ham-Egg-Brie Strudel 56

Honey Granola with Yogurt 42

Honey-Wheat Pancakes.............................. 53

Jumbo Lump Crabmeat with Potato
Pancakes, Mango and Baby
Greens....................................... 64

Leg of Lamb with Mustard and Mint
Sauce.. 146

Lemon Chicken with Moroccan
Olives, Pine Nuts, Toasted Garlic &
Couscous 70

Light 'n' Crisp Waffles.................................. 49

Macaroni Gratin 101

Mesquite-Grilled Tiger Prawns with Pesto,
Cannellini Beans, Grilled Radicchio,
Fennel and Confit Tomatoes 74

Moroccan Chicken Turnovers.................... 66

Moroccan Stir-Fry 112

Phyllo Breakfast Spirals............................. 46

Pork Tenderloin with Molasses, Bacon
    and Porcini Vinaigrette 121

Real Pan-Fried Chicken 90

Roasted Sweet Potato & Hoisin Lettuce
    Wraps 117

Seared Beef Tenderloin with
    Horseradish-Rosemary Cream 130

Seared Tilapia with Black Olive
    Salsa.. 108

Shrimp, Goat Cheese & Leek Tortilla 80

Skillet Tuscan Pork with Fresh
    Tomatoes 92

Smoked Salmon Hash Browns 48

Steak al Forno.. 28

Strawberry-Apricot Barbecue Cornish
    Hens... 27

Triple Blueberry Waffles 38

anchego Cheese Croquettes................. 138

lango-Banana Foster 32

lascarpone-Mint Ice Cream, Fresh Figs
    and Vanilla-Lemon Syrup 26

ashed Sweet Potatoes with Cilantro
    and Lime 144

esquite-Grilled Tiger Prawns with Pesto,
    Cannellini Beans, Grilled Radicchio,
    Fennel and Confit Tomatoes 74

lini Cherry Kugel.. 144

lini Crab and Goat Cheese Empanadas
    with Mango Chutney.................................. 114

ini Gingerbread Wheat Cakes 68

lini Smoked Salmon Latkes 134

lorning Mocha Smoothie 34

oroccan Chicken Turnovers....................... 66

loroccan Stir-Fry 112

lushroom Stuffing 143

utty Toffee Ice Cream Cake..................... 22

live Tapenade... 24

ne-Bite Burgers.. 124

eppery Green Beans 150

hyllo Breakfast Spirals 46

Pork

Beef Rib Roast with Mushroom-Bacon
    Sauce... 152

Bratwurst Skillet Breakfast 52

Chorizo & Artichoke Kabobs with
    Mustard Vinaigrette.................................. 62

Eggs Benedict with Asparagus &
    Crab... 57

Goat Cheese Stuffed Figs............................ 58

Ham & Egg Breakfast Panini 44

Ham-Egg-Brie Strudel 56

Little Ribs in Paprika Sauce........................ 96

Phyllo Breakfast Spirals................................ 46

Pork Tenderloin with Molasses, Bacon
    and Porcini Vinaigrette 121

Real Pan-Fried Chicken 90

Skillet Tuscan Pork with Fresh
    Tomatoes 92

Pork Tenderloin with Molasses, Bacon
    and Porcini Vinaigrette.............................. 121

Pumpkin & Parmesan Twice-Baked
    Potatoes 147

Real Pan-Fried Chicken................................ 90

Roasted Sweet Potato & Hoisin Lettuce
    Wraps... 117

Roasted Sweet Potatoes with Apples &
    Raisins 98

Roasted Vegetable Salad with Capers
    and Walnuts 94

Salads

Calamari Salad... 122

Fresh Spinach-Strawberry Salad 82

Grilled Potato Salad 16

Grilled Vegetable Salad with Feta
    and Olives 21

Mesquite-Grilled Tiger Prawns with Pesto,
    Cannellini Beans, Grilled Radicchio,
    Fennel and Confit Tomatoes 74

Roasted Vegetable Salad with Capers
    and Walnuts 94

Thai Cabbage-Apple Slaw.......................... 14

Warm Crab & Fingerling Potato Salad
    with Horseradish Crème Fraîche
    and Baby Red Oak Lettuce 129

157

Savory Bread Pudding with Asparagus and Dried Tomatoes 151

Seafood

Almond-Coated Scallops 76

Calamari Salad 122

Chilled Avocado & Gazpacho Soup 20

Citrus-Marinated Atlantic Salmon with Potato Blinis and Garden Greens 78

Crab-Stuffed Portobello Mushrooms 116

Eggs Benedict with Asparagus & Crab 57

Fish Bites with Romesco Sauce 110

Garlic Shrimp Casserole 97

Jumbo Lump Crabmeat with Potato Pancakes, Mango and Baby Greens 64

Mesquite-Grilled Tiger Prawns with Pesto, Cannellini Beans, Grilled Radicchio, Fennel and Confit Tomatoes 74

Mini Crab and Goat Cheese Empanadas with Mango Chutney 114

Mini Smoked Salmon Latkes 134

Seared Tilapia with Black Olive Salsa 108

Shrimp and Scallop Tapas 77

Shrimp, Goat Cheese & Leek Tortilla 80

Smoked Salmon Hash Browns 48

Tangerine Tequila Shrimp 8

Warm Crab & Fingerling Potato Salad with Horseradish Crème Fraîche and Baby Red Oak Lettuce 129

Seared Beef Tenderloin with Horseradish-Rosemary Cream 130

Seared Tilapia with Black Olive Salsa 108

Shortbread-Crusted Cheesecake with Raspberry-Ginger Sauce 148

Shrimp and Scallop Tapas 77

Shrimp, Goat Cheese & Leek Tortilla 80

Side Dishes

Brussels Sprouts with Walnuts 136

Calamari Salad 122

Chilled Avocado & Gazpacho Soup 20

Curried Pumpkin-Apple Soup 132

Fruited Corn Pudding 142

Grilled Potato Salad 16

Grilled Vegetable Salad with Feta and Olives 2

Honey-Lemon Green & Yellow Beans 100

Macaroni Gratin 10

Manchego Cheese Croquettes 138

Mashed Sweet Potatoes with Cilantro and Lime 144

Mini Cherry Kugel 144

Mushroom Stuffing 143

Peppery Green Beans 150

Phyllo Breakfast Spirals 46

Pumpkin & Parmesan Twice-Baked Potatoes 147

Roasted Sweet Potatoes with Apples & Raisins 98

Roasted Vegetable Salad with Capers and Walnuts 94

Savory Bread Pudding with Asparagus and Dried Tomatoes 15

Shrimp, Goat Cheese & Leek Tortilla 80

Smoked Salmon Hash Browns 48

Thai Cabbage-Apple Slaw 14

Tri-Color Cauliflower 86

Twice-Baked Potatoes with Sun-Dried Tomatoes 128

Skillet Tuscan Pork with Fresh Tomatoes 92

Smoked Salmon Hash Browns 48

Snacks

Baked Brie with Nut Crust 99

Cheesecake Cookie Bars 104

Chocolate Hazelnut Cupcakes 72

Chocolate Waffle Cookies 105

Chorizo & Artichoke Kabobs with Mustard Vinaigrette 62

Citrus-Marinated Atlantic Salmon with Potato Blinis and Garden Greens 78

Crab-Stuffed Portobello Mushrooms 116

158

Cranberry Orange Pumpkin Scones
 with Whipped Maple Butter 36

Easy Raspberry-Peach Danish 54

Edamame Hummus...6

Fish Bites with Romesco Sauce 110

Goat Cheese Stuffed Figs........................ 58

Ham & Egg Breakfast Panini 44

Honey Granola with Yogurt 42

Hot & Sweet Deviled Eggs 120

Jumbo Lump Crabmeat with Potato
 Pancakes, Mango and Baby
 Greens 64

Little Ribs in Paprika Sauce........................ 96

Manchego Cheese Croquettes 138

Mini Crab and Goat Cheese Empanadas
 with Mango Chutney............................. 114

Mini Cherry Kugel 144

Mini Gingerbread Wheat Cakes.............. 68

Mini Smoked Salmon Latkes.................. 134

Moroccan Chicken Turnovers.................. 66

Olive Tapenade... 24

One-Bite Burgers 124

Roasted Sweet Potato & Hoisin Lettuce
 Wraps 117

Shrimp and Scallop Tapas......................... 77

Shrimp, Goat Cheese & Leek
 Tortilla...80

Smoked Salmon Hash Browns................. 48

Tangerine Tequila Shrimp............................8

Wine Biscuits.. 60

Steak al Forno 28

Strawberry-Apricot Barbecue Cornish
 Hens 27

Tangerine-Tequila Shrimp.................................8

Thai Cabbage-Apple Slaw 14

Tri-Color Cauliflower 86

Triple Blueberry Waffles.................................. 38

Twice-Baked Potatoes with Sun-Dried
 Tomatoes.. 128

Vegetarian Dishes
 Baked Brie with Nut Crust.......................... 99

 Breakfast Rice Pudding............................... 40

 Brussels Sprouts with Walnuts 136

Chilled Avocado & Gazpacho
 Soup.. 20

Cranberry Orange Pumpkin Scones
 with Whipped Maple Butter 36

Curried Pumpkin-Apple Soup................ 132

Edamame Hummus...6

Fresh Spinach-Strawberry Salad 82

Fruited Corn Pudding 142

Grilled Potato Salad 16

Honey Granola with Yogurt 42

Honey-Lemon Green & Yellow
 Beans 100

Honey-Wheat Pancakes............................. 53

Hot & Sweet Deviled Eggs 120

Light 'n' Crisp Waffles 49

Macaroni Gratin 101

Manchego Cheese Croquettes 138

Mashed Sweet Potatoes with
 Cilantro and Lime 144

Mini Cherry Kugel 144

Olive Tapenade... 24

Peppery Green Beans 150

Phyllo Breakfast Spirals.............................. 46

Pumpkin & Parmesan Twice-Baked
 Potatoes..147

Roasted Sweet Potato & Hoisin Lettuce
 Wraps 117

Roasted Vegetable Salad with Capers
 and Walnuts 94

Savory Bread Pudding with Asparagus
 and Dried Tomatoes.............................. 151

Thai Cabbage-Apple Slaw........................ 14

Tri-Color Cauliflower 86

Triple Blueberry Waffles............................. 38

Twice-Baked Potatoes with Sun-Dried
 Tomatoes... 128

Warm Crab & Fingerling Potato Salad
 with Horseradish Crème Fraîche
 and Baby Red Oak Lettuce..................... 129

Whoopie Pies 84

Wine Biscuits 60

METRIC CONVERSION CHART

VOLUME MEASUREMENTS (dry)

$1/8$ teaspoon = 0.5 mL
$1/4$ teaspoon = 1 mL
$1/2$ teaspoon = 2 mL
$3/4$ teaspoon = 4 mL
1 teaspoon = 5 mL
1 tablespoon = 15 mL
2 tablespoons = 30 mL
$1/4$ cup = 60 mL
$1/3$ cup = 75 mL
$1/2$ cup = 125 mL
$2/3$ cup = 150 mL
$3/4$ cup = 175 mL
1 cup = 250 mL
2 cups = 1 pint = 500 mL
3 cups = 750 mL
4 cups = 1 quart = 1 L

VOLUME MEASUREMENTS (fluid)

1 fluid ounce (2 tablespoons) = 30 mL
4 fluid ounces ($1/2$ cup) = 125 mL
8 fluid ounces (1 cup) = 250 mL
12 fluid ounces ($1 1/2$ cups) = 375 mL
16 fluid ounces (2 cups) = 500 mL

WEIGHTS (mass)

$1/2$ ounce = 15 g
1 ounce = 30 g
3 ounces = 90 g
4 ounces = 120 g
8 ounces = 225 g
10 ounces = 285 g
12 ounces = 360 g
16 ounces = 1 pound = 450 g

DIMENSIONS

$1/16$ inch = 2 mm
$1/8$ inch = 3 mm
$1/4$ inch = 6 mm
$1/2$ inch = 1.5 cm
$3/4$ inch = 2 cm
1 inch = 2.5 cm

OVEN TEMPERATURES

250°F = 120°C
275°F = 140°C
300°F = 150°C
325°F = 160°C
350°F = 180°C
375°F = 190°C
400°F = 200°C
425°F = 220°C
450°F = 230°C

BAKING PAN AND DISH EQUIVALENTS

Utensil	Size in Inches	Size in Centimeters	Volume	Metric Volume
Baking or Cake Pan (square or rectangular)	8×8×2	20×20×5	8 cups	2 L
	9×9×2	23×23×5	10 cups	2.5 L
	13×9×2	33×23×5	12 cups	3 L
Loaf Pan	8½×4½×2½	21×11×6	6 cups	1.5 L
	9×9×3	23×13×7	8 cups	2 L
Round Layer Cake Pan	8×1½	20×4	4 cups	1 L
	9×1½	23×4	5 cups	1.25 L
Pie Plate	8×1½	20×4	4 cups	1 L
	9×1½	23×4	5 cups	1.25 L
Baking Dish or Casserole			1 quart/4 cups	1 L
			1½ quart/6 cups	1.5 L
			2 quart/8 cups	2 L
			3 quart/12 cups	3 L